Macdonald Illustrated war studies

German Airborne Troops
British Airborne Troops
Carrier Fighters
Hitler's Elite – *Leibstandarte SS*
World War II Fighter Conflict

Forthcoming:
The E-Boat Threat
The U-Boat Hunters
World War II Bomber

THE U.S. STRATEGIC BOMBER

Roger Freeman
E U.S. STRATEGIC BOMBER
Macdonald and Jane's: London

First published in 1975
by Macdonald and Jane's
(Macdonald & Co. (Publishers) Ltd.)
Paulton House, 8 Shepherdess Walk
London N1 7LW

Typesetting, Bedford Typesetters Ltd
Made and Printed in Great Britain by
Morrison & Gibb Ltd
London and Edinburgh

ISBN 0 356 08096 x

Layout and make-up: Michael Jarvis
Maps and diagrams: Norman Ottaway

Contents

Glossary

Introduction

This book aims to provide a concise account of the evolution, development and record of strategic bombardment by the United States Army's air arm. The bomber as a decisive weapon, and the doctrine governing its employment were unique among combatants of World War II and had an effect reaching far beyond that conflict.

Heavy bomber operations were not all for a strategic purpose and in this account the concern is principally with operations meeting strategic directives. Often the classification of an operation as tactical or strategic was arbitrary. Operations undertaken for tactical reasons could also have a strategic effect and vice versa. To define the differences, it could be said that the tactical bomber was committed to supporting ground forces, with targets ranging from troop concentrations in the vicinity of battle lines to ports of supply perhaps 200 miles distant. The strategic bomber was employed in attacks on sources of production and vital facilities in the enemy home or occupied lands, to force the issue unassociated with any land or sea campaign. This singular ideal of a strategic air offensive was not achieved in Europe nor wholly in the very heavy bomber campaign against the Japanese homeland.

The United States' strategic air forces were the 8th, 15th and 20th; they conducted bombardment on an unprecedented scale with 300 squadrons and 5,000 aircraft at their combined peaks, a vast wartime investment for an untried doctrine. Instrumental in this effort was the undeterred faith in offensive airpower of the air leaders. Several personalities were involved and it is surprising that the small, suppressed air service of the 'twenties fostered so many brilliant tacticians and commanders of the 'forties.

Roger A. Freeman   January 1975

Acknowledgements

The following persons provided information and material or assisted in other ways in the preparation of this book: Robert L. Cavanagh, James Denmark, Dr James H. Doolittle, James H. Farmer, Ian MacTaggart, Merle Olmsted, Norman Ottaway, Ken Ranson, William G. Robertie and Kenn C. Rust. Bruce Robertson gave considerable editorial assistance and Jean Freeman coped with the tedious task of typing the final manuscript. To all I express my sincere thanks. The use of facilities at the Imperial War Museum, Air Force Museum, Third Air Force Press Office and USAF Aerospace Audio Visual Service is also gratefully acknowledged.

Select Bibliography

Army Air Forces in World War II, Craven & Gate
AAF Reference Histories, including 10, 18, 22 & 70
Guide to The AAF
AAF Statistical Digest
The Air Plan that Defeated Hitler. Brigadier General Haywood S. Hansell
Global Mission. General H. H. Arnold
History of the United States Air Force 1907–1957
U.S. Strategic Bombing Survey, various reports
Air Force Magazine
The Airpower Historian

In 1920 an
American-built
bombing aircraft
was rare enough in
the western states
to be a curiosity.
This Martin MB-1
was put on public
display at
Crissy Field,
San Francisco.
*Randolph Brant
Collection*

1. The Doctrine and the Weapon

Development of the strategic bombing concept and its proposed application through daylight precision attack.

Once organised aerial bombing started early in the 1914–1918 war, it was a logical step that the targets for missiles dropped from early military aircraft would extend from the battlefield to the lines of communication to harass troops in billets and blow up munition dumps behind the front. With technical advances bringing larger bombs, increased engine power and more sophisticated instruments the ultimate step was taken to seek out the sources of production on which modern warfare depends. The Wright brothers' invention developed apace during the war and before the end multi-engined bombers were capable of lifting a ton of bombs and delivering them 300 miles. A strategist's dream became reality.

The Germans made the first organised bombing raid on Compiègne in 1914 and attacked their enemy's capital, London, with Zeppelins in 1915 and multi-engined bombers later in the war. The British Royal Naval Air Service established a Wing in France for strategic bombing in 1916, but the conflicting interests of the Royal Flying Corp's tactical use of aircraft caused inter-service conflict, which led to a governmental decision to amalgamate these forces in April 1918 into a completely new service – the Royal Air Force. In June 1918 another major step was the setting up of an Independent Force to carry the war to sources of military production and the services that nurtured it – a mission of strategic bombing. For the next five months, until an armistice was signed, the Independent Force used large Handley Page bombers to carry out raids which, whenever possible, were to centres of war industry, particularly steel-making plants in western Germany. The commander of this force, Major General Sir Hugh Trenchard, was convinced that the aeroplane was the offensive weapon of the future.

The United States did not come into the war until April 1917 and her participation in aerial hostilities was brief, but meritorious. That there was a significant aerial contribution at all was perhaps in part due to the agitation of Colonel William E. Mitchell, a U.S. Army officer originally sent to Europe as an observer. Mitchell had been connected with the small aviation section of the U.S. Signal Corps from whence his enthusiasm had grown for furthering the aeroplane as a military machine. Subsequently given a field command of flying units behind the French front in the spring of 1918, he distinguished himself in combat.

Although the first American air squadrons were not committed to the Front until April 1918, a force of 740 aircraft – including 120 designated as bomber types – were operational by the Armistice in November. Of the forty-five combat squadrons, six were equipped with day bombers and one with night bombers. The bombers' contribution was 215 raids dispensing 255,000 lb of explosive. Their raids, however, were mainly tactical support of ground forces. The American air commanders were interested in the strategic operations of the British Independent Force, particularly Mitchell who was greatly influenced by Trenchard. Mitchell gained the approval of his Air Service superiors – Brigadier General M. M. Patrick, Chief of Air Service, AEF, and Brigadier General B. D. Foulois, Chief of Air Service, 1st Army – of the American Expeditionary Force, to form and train a U.S. element to participate with the Independent Force. To this end the manufacture of Handley Page bombers was undertaken in the U.S.A. and crews were instructed in their handling. However, hostilities ceased before this contribution saw any action.

Mitchell's Endeavours and Achievements

The U.S. Army Air Service readily absorbed much of the doctrine formulated by their Allies, particularly the Royal Air Force, the first independent military service established to operate aircraft. American air officers serving in Europe, having experienced or seen the air weapon in action, were imbued with the desire to see the United States create a similar service independent of the U.S. Army. The Army General Staff, however, found nothing in the experiences of World War I to justify such a step. The aeroplane, like the tank, was to them simply a new weapon to be employed in support of infantry and artillery. Moreover, the United States had returned to an isolationist policy with the role of the armed forces limited to defence. The physical barriers of the Atlantic and Pacific were deemed obstacles enough to deter sea invasion from another continent and land neighbours north and south did not present any major threat. Thus a comparatively small army would suffice with oceanic defence in the hands of a strong navy, particularly in view of the U.S. territories and protectorates in the Pacific – notably Hawaii and the Philippines.

In 1919 the United States carried out massive demobilisation after a war in which a great many Americans believed their country should never have become involved. The Air Service was reduced from nearly 200,000 men to less than 10,000 by the spring of 1920 leaving two dozen first-line squadrons supporting the various Army corps areas. The bombardment mission was left to a solitary group, the 2nd Bombardment Group, formed from an organisation which had served in France. Despite this indication of how little the Army regarded the importance of its air arm, the desire for an autonomous force persisted among the aviators. Foremost among these was the flamboyant and voluble Brigadier General 'Billy' Mitchell who, on his return from Europe, was appointed in March 1919 as Director of Military Aeronautics under the Director of Air Service. An energetic public orator and able writer, Mitchell used these talents to propound his passion for air power and his conviction that it introduced a completely new mode of warfare requiring an organisation separate from the traditional forces. His pronouncements along these lines were resented by many of the traditionalists in Army, Navy and government. Nor were all Air Service officers his friends; some with similar ideals felt his swashbuckling ways impeded progress by antagonising those who held power.

In his new post Mitchell was able to promote technical projects to advance military aviation, but the principal obstacle was an acute lack of funds. The Air Service had to make use of the large surplus of aircraft and equipment from war production. Combat aircraft were predominantly of European design, the major exception being a twin-engine aircraft from Glenn L. Martin originally ordered as a reconnaissance machine with bombing capability. Showing influence of Handley Page and Caproni designs, produced under licence in the U.S.A. in 1918, the slightly smaller Martin had a comparable performance and was a better aircraft. Endurance, however, was only about half that of the foreign types, giving a practical radius of action of some 175 miles. At first known as the GMB (Glenn Martin Bomber), and later as the MB-1 (Martin Bomber No 1), the machine was powered by Liberty water-cooled engines suspended between the two 71-foot span main planes. A crew of three was standard: pilot and two gunners, one of whom doubled as bombardier. Five rifle-calibre machine guns were provided for defence and the aircraft could lift a maximum bomb load of 1,040 lb. Only nine Martins were delivered by Armistice Day and thereafter funds for new equipment were curtailed. The desire to foster an indigenous efficient bomber was partly responsible for twenty advanced versions of the MB-1 promptly ordered from Glenn Martin when the Army Reorganisation Act of June 1920 gave the Air Service limited funds for and control of research, development and procurement of aircraft and associated equipment. In addition to refinements to engines and undercarriage the new Martin, the MB-2, had strengthened and slightly larger wing area to give greater lift to raise the maximum bomb load to 1,791 lb. Heavier than its predecessor and still powered by surplus wartime Liberty engines, the aircraft's performance suffered, but for the first time the Air Service had a capable bomber of indigenous design.

Through Mitchell's agitation, a prototype long-range night bomber was also funded as an experimental project in 1920; for which the campaigning general had high hopes in giving practical demonstration of his assertions about the value of the far-ranging bomber. Designed by Walter Barling and built by a New Jersey firm, this giant triplane of 120 feet span, with two tailplanes and four fins and rudders, powered by six Liberty engines, was supported by four undercarriage rigs with a total of ten wheels. Designated XNBL-1 (Experimental Night Bomber Long-range) it was not ready to fly until the summer of 1923. Weight was in excess of 27,000 lb empty in contrast to MB-2's 7,000 lb, and though capable of taking to the air with an additional 15,000 lb in bombs, fuel and crew, performance was inferior to the MB-2. If the 5,000 lb maximum bomb load was carried, the reduction in fuel restricted the lumbering goliath to a mere 85 miles radius of action. In complete mockery of its designation it did not out-range the smaller MB-2 carrying the same load. The problems of the Barling were many, but principally poor power/weight ratio.

The existence and capabilities of the big aircraft were the subject of exaggerated news publicity and the Air Service did not detract from this; but the truth was known in the War Department where the expenditure of more than $350,000 received critical assessment. Thereafter the Army kept a closer watch on the Air Service expenditure on prototypes. The Barling was abandoned in 1925, by which time it had come to be known in some military circles as 'Mitchell's Folly'. Mitchell, too, had by then fallen from favour with the War Department. Had it not been for his war record and high standing with the public, firmer and earlier action might have been taken by his superiors to quell his pronouncements which were frequently provocative and embarrassing to the Army hierarchy.

A notable assertion of Mitchell's was the capability of the bombing aeroplane to attack and sink large naval vessels – an assertion hotly refuted by an indignant Navy. Thus antagonised, the Navy undertook some tests of its own but these were inconclusive as far as Mitchell's canvassing was concerned. His persistence led to Congressional approval for a test involving bombers against capitulated ships of the German Navy that were to be scrapped. Navy aircraft were also involved but it was Air Service MB-2s that were primarily responsible for first finishing off the destroyer *G-102* with 300 lb bombs, then sinking the cruiser *Frankfurt* with 600 pounders and, finally, despatching the heavily compartmented battleship *Ostfriesland* with 1,000 lb and 2,000 lb bombs. The warships were anchored off Virginia Capes, some 97 miles from the bombers' base at Langley Field. The bombings were conducted between 13th and 21st July 1921, followed by further tests in September when the Martins were again successful, sinking the obsolete battleship *Alabama* with a direct hit by a 2,000 lb bomb. These heavy high explosive missiles had been specially made for the tests and Mitchell had designs on even larger ones for his bombers, with work on a 4,000 pounder* in hand.

While funds to the Air Service were cut drastically after 1921, the spectacular warship bombings impressed Mitchell's superiors sufficiently to allow another 110 Martin bombers to be ordered, all of which were manufactured by contractors and not the parent firm to help keep the industry alive. A new designation, NBS-1 (Nigh Bomber Short-range) was given to these aircraft that would provide the principal bombing capability for five years. As the designation reveals, night operation was envisaged, Royal Air Force war experience having shown that large aircraft had a much better chance of evading fighters under the cover of darkness.

Meanwhile, reacting to the bombing tests, the Navy averred that had the vessels been under way evasive action would have been taken so in no way had the battleship's supremacy been challenged. Even the Army General Staff appears to have concurred with this view; the fact that the ships had been destroyed by assault from the air did not bring any government reappraisal of Air Service status. If the Navy conceded little publicly, the lessons from these tests were not lost on its tacticians for from this time forth aviation became an increasingly important element of the fleet. It may also be observed that Mitchell's prodding and the warship bombings engendered a certain hostility within the Navy towards the upstart Army air arm and its lineal successors, that persisted for more than thirty years.

For Mitchell, the results only affirmed his conviction that the aeroplane could change the pattern of war and this acted as a spur to his bold pronouncements on air power. He was not always consistent in his views but his broad aim, while affirming that fighter aviation was essential, was that strategic bombardment would decide the issue in future wars.

Further successful bombing tests were conducted against old warships in

---

* A 4,300 lb bomb was first lifted by a Handley Page and dropped on the Aberdeen Proving Grounds, Maryland on 28th September 1921.

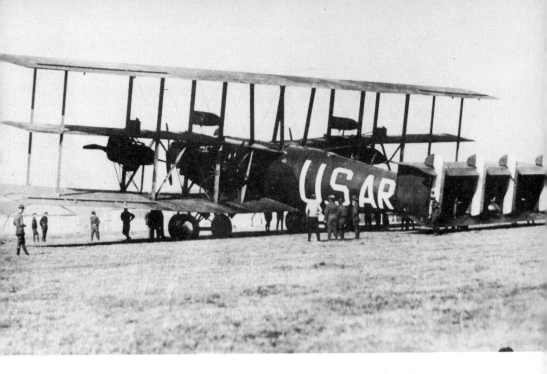

1923, but neither these nor Mitchell's activities brought any change to the outlook of the War Department. Indeed, the reverse was the case; the War Department's displeasure was conveyed to Mitchell in April 1925 when he was given a posting that was in effect demotion. His public outbursts becoming even more scathing of the policy direction of both Army and Navy, eventually provoked the authorities to court martial him. Found guilty and suspended for five years, he resigned the service in 1926.

At least Mitchell's activities and martyrdom resulted in a majority of his fellow officers, sympathetic to his ideas, becoming hardened canvassers for an independent air arm. If less willing to sacrifice their military careers, by antagonising their superiors, they were nonetheless active in the campaign. The quest for autonomy would prompt consideration by various government authorised boards and committees during the next decade, but the traditionalists of the Army hierarchy still held sway and most findings were to the effect that the mission of air units was in support of the ground forces. The recommendations of one board of enquiry indirectly resulting from Mitchell's demise were incorporated in the Air Corps Act of July 1926. They introduced a new title – Air Corps – which was considered more fitting than Air Service, and a promise of a five-year boost to personnel and equipment.

Interested spectators lend scale to the U.S. Army's first aerial giant, the Whiteman XNBL-1, popularly known as the Barling Bomber. An awe-inspiring spectacle in flight, it was a dismal failure as a heavy bomber. USMC/ A. Thometz

Technical Progress 1926-1931

In the mid-'twenties most of the Army's aircraft were still drawn from World War I surpluses while those few new combat types purchased since the Armistice were all powered with the Liberty engine, a legacy of wartime mass production with large numbers still in store. Funds were forthcoming for a replacement for the wood and fabric NBS-1s which had deteriorated badly, the choice being narrowed to a twin-engine biplane made by the Keystone Aircraft Company of Bristol, Pennsylvania, designated LB-5 by the Air Corps. The designation LB stood for Light Bomber, showing that there were still aspirations for a heavier type. Employing a fabric-covered metal steel tube frame, the aircraft was of similar size and weight to the NBS-1 and, because Libertys also produced the power, of like performance. A sturdy machine, it offered little advance, and was bought principally because of its low cost, $28,000 each – only $4,000 more than the old Martins cost seven years previously.

One of the chief factors limiting performance was the adherence to the Liberty engine, with its maximum rating of 420 horse-power. Overheating was a constant problem but as the engine was cheap with ample spares available, manufacturers chose it to hold down the price of their aircraft. This gave no encouragement to engine manufacturers and in the end an Order of Congress was made prohibiting the acceptance of any new aircraft with Libertys. Ironically, it was the U.S. Navy, despite its implied aversion to the aeroplane, that encouraged the development of engines that would eventually predominate in Army aircraft. The inherent cooling problems and difficult maintenance of the Liberty made it highly unsuitable for aircraft operating from carriers and caused the Navy to take interest in air-cooled engines.

Air-cooled engines with cylinders radiating from the crankcase were devised during World War I but not until the 1920s did they become a practical proposition through refinements in cooling fins. Most successful designs were those of Pratt and Whitney and of Wright, which by the end of the 'twenties were powering all Navy combat aircraft. Not only did these engines dispense with the troublesome water mixture coolant and weighty radiators, but they were considerably lighter and easier to maintain than other types. Moreover, by 1927 the Wright R-1750 radial could develop 536 horse-power and was reliable enough to be selected to power a further order for Keystones. All told, 210 Keystone bombers of various designations were ordered between 1927 and 1932 and used to re-equip the 2nd Bombardment Group's squadrons at Langley and to truly establish the 7th Bombardment Group, based in California, as the west coast bomber force; others went to squadrons of the 5th Composite Group in Hawaii and the 6th Composite in the Panama Canal zone.

In their ultimate form (B-6A*) the Keystones had a top speed of 120 mph, a ceiling of 14,000 feet, a 180 miles' radius of action with the 2,200 lb maximum bomb load. While this range could be substantially greater with a smaller load – in excess of 800 miles' radius of action without bombs – these aircraft were of little value in advancing the doctrines of offensive bombardment, still being actively advocated by the Air Corps. In terms of practical performance, the Keystones showed little advantage over the NBS-1s of 1922. Even the defensive armament was a legacy of World War I with the same open nose and dorsal Lewis gun emplacements with the field of fire of the latter handicapped by the tail assembly.

Better defence and performance was exhibited by the Curtiss B-2 Condor

---

* The Air Corps introduced standardised aircraft designations in the late 1920s in which bomber types had a single letter B prefix in a numbering system starting at 1, with a further qualifying prefix X for Experimental or Y for Service Test.

The Keystone era: a flight of LB-5As of the 5th Group patrolling Hawaian waters. *Gross G. Risedorph*

offered to the Air Corps in 1928. But the Air Corps selection board with limited funds chose Keystones in quantity in preference to quality. Curtiss were, however, given a small contract for twelve B-2s. These aircraft were at least 10 mph faster than the latest Keystones and offered more than double the range. The Condor featured an attempt to improve the tail defence with the siting of a machine gun post in the rear of each engine nacelle. The engines, also of Curtiss design, were the first liquid-cooled types in squadron aircraft since the Libertys were barred. Although powerful with a 633 horsepower rating, they proved troublesome and were a barrier to further orders in place of Keystones. The gain in bombardment strength during the expansion period 1927 to mid-1932 was twelve squadrons of Keystones and one of Condors.

If the multi-engined bomber had seemingly made little progress since the end of World War I there was no lack of endeavour within the resources of the Air Service/Air Corps to advance technology, particularly by the Engineering Division of Dayton, Ohio. Charged with experimentation and research in military aviation, this Division had been set up in 1917 to prepare British and Italian designs for production, and progressed to the testing of all Army aircraft and equipment, also engaging in practical development projects. Incorporated in the newly created Material Division of the Air Corps in 1926, the establishment moved from its original station at McCook Field to larger facilities at Wright Field a few miles away, late the following year. Both the Army and Navy also drew on the services of the National Advisory Committee on Aeronautics (NACA), a government sponsored institution set up in 1915 to undertake 'scientific research on the fundamental problems of flight'. There were also other national agencies and commercial companies which co-operated with Wright Field.

In the immediate post-war period, many of the devices utilised in World War II were being investigated or were in the early stages of development. In April 1919 over McCook Field, Leslie Irving made the first jump from an aircraft with a free backpack parachute, later adopted as standard by the Air Corps. The designer, Floyd Smith, piloted the DH-4 used on this occa-

15

sion. In this same year research was also being conducted on variable and reversible pitch propellers, leakproof fuel tanks and pressurised cabins.

Engine superchargers for high-altitude flight merited special attention. These compressed rarified air to a density equal to that at sea level, preventing engines being starved of oxygen at high altitude and raising by several thousand feet the ceiling at which aircraft could work efficiently. Basically a supercharger consisted of an air compressing impeller driven either mechanically through gears, or from engine exhaust gases working a turbine wheel. A promising example of the latter type, known as the turbo-supercharger, was developed by the General Electric Company in 1918 and installed on a Packard-LePere biplane fighter at McCook the following year. Several high altitude flights were made with this machine, including an official world altitude record of 33,113 feet on 27th February 1920 by Major R. W. Schroeder. Primitive oxygen equipment had already been developed and high altitude flights gave impetus to further research and development in this field. In the summer of 1920 a series of high altitude parachute jumps were made over McCook to discover the physiological effects of a descent from oxygen-mask heights, Lieutenant J. H. Wilson making a successful jump from 19,800 feet on 8th June.

The turbo-supercharged LePere was clawing higher into the stratosphere and using it on 28th September 1921 Lieutenant J. A. Macready raised the world altitude record to 34,508 feet. That December Lieutenant L. Wade took an MB-2 with turbos installed to 25,600 feet, nearly 16,000 feet above the type's normal ceiling. From this supercharged Martin, Captain A. W. Stevens made a record high altitude parachute jump at 24,206 feet on 12th June the following year.

The superchargers were cumbersome and not without over-heating effects on engines, but the chief obstacle to their use was the inefficiency of the fixed-blade propellers as the aircraft climbed higher. The pitch could be adjusted on the ground for high altitude flight for experiments but this was not practical on service aircraft; a propeller was needed where the pitch of the blades could be varied in flight to allow for the reduced air density at high altitudes. Because of these problems the plan to operate MB-2s with superchargers was dropped although some were delivered with these installations.

Research into airframe design was not neglected by Wright Field. The use of aluminium sheet skin by the German Junkers firm in 1918 prompted development of the process at McCook Field where a prototype monoplane, the Gallaudet DB-1B, became in June 1923 the first all-metal aircraft built and flown in the United States. There were many other technical advances, those detailed giving an indication of the effort to extend flight into the stratosphere, and assist bomber development. Although success was often proclaimed because something had been achieved, the equipment involved was often inadequate or far from dependable. At this time the results of these high altitude experiments were not pursued to meet a directive for the development of high altitude bombardment. The current bomb sights limited accurate attack to a few thousand feet. Again ironically, it was the U.S. Navy that fostered the instrument which was to be of inestimable value in the development of high altitude bombing.

At the end of World War I the Navy became interested in a bomb sight

designed by a civilian engineer, Mr C. L. Norden. This sight was developed and used in Navy seaplanes during the 1920s. In 1930 Norden produced a new advanced design and this, the Navy Mark XV, was used in a test against an obsolete warship in October 1931. Army Air Corps observers were so impressed that they requested a number of these sights which were initially tried out in December that same year at Rockwell, California, where Curtiss B-2s of the 11th Bomb Squadron carried out highly successful trials from 6,000, 9,000 and 12,000 feet. Finding the sight far and away superior to their own C and D models, the Air Corps procured a further 78 Nordens in 1933. The Norden was a very sophisticated instrument employing gyroscopes and a mechanism that automatically computed various factors so that when set up correctly the actual release of bombs was made electrically at the predetermined spot. Not only did the sight greatly simplify the job of the bombardier but it gave a very high degree of accuracy.

Bomb sights and other technical achievements to further the value of the bomber could little enhance the strategic potential while the aircraft in the Army Air Corps squadrons were so deficient in performance. Endurance with payload was the factor which committed the Keystones to tactical support of the ground forces, whatever Air Corps theorists might wish.

Best of the Air Corps' biplane bombers, the B-2 Condor equipped the 11th BS, 7th BG, during the early 'thirties. Their first-line service was nearly over when this photo of air and ground crew, lined up for morning inspection at March Field, California, was taken in February 1934. *USAAC/ R. Louden*

Development of Doctrine

In the early 'thirties Air Corps interest in offensive bombardment was mainly centred in the Tactical School at Maxwell Field, Alabama. This seminary had originally been established at Langley Field, Virginia, in October 1920 as the Air Service Field Officers' School; later the name was changed to Air Service Tactical School and again in 1926 to Air Corps Tactical School, remaining at this location until 1931 when the move to Maxwell was made. As the title implies, the purpose was to teach the tactics of employing the aeroplane in war. Policy behind tactics was largely formulated by the faculty instructors developing ideas.

For the first decade following World War I the school manuals were influenced by Air Service tactical experience in that campaign where missions in direct support of the Army were the prime consideration, but the possibility of independent air operations in some future war were acknowledged, if rather ambiguously. Since these manuals could come under the eyes of those outside the Air Corps, they were couched in careful terms. The opinions expressed by the faculty were less reserved. 'Billy' Mitchell had been the Air Service's colourful visionary who focused attention upon aircraft's use in a new field of military operations, but he was far from alone in his beliefs in strategic bombardment. It was to be expected that war veterans, continuing Army careers, would eventually gravitate to a post in the Tactical School. Men with bombardment backgrounds came to head the section of the school devoted to bomber tactics while the pursuit and observation sections drew chiefly on men who had extensive practical knowledge of these missions. They were usually dedicated exponents of their particular aerial art and so stimulated a fighter versus bomber controversy within the School. The pursuit or fighter had emerged the dominant type of aircraft in World War I, achieved by its ability to pursue and destroy slower and less manoeuvrable bomber and observation types.

Captain Harold L. George's appointment as the Tactical School's Chief of Bombardment Section in 1931, gave the initial impetus to the formulation of a strategic bombing doctrine. George had flown DH-4 bombers with the AEF in France and had piloted a Martin during the warship bombing tests of 1921. With this practical grounding he followed Mitchell's concepts of the offensive value of the air weapon. While it would be wrong to attribute the evolution of the USAAC's doctrine of strategic bombardment to him alone, for Major Robert Olds, Hugh Kneer and other predecessors were dedicated to bomber supremacy, he was the first to state a firm precept, no doubt aided in his convictions by technical advances that occurred in the early 'thirties. The precept assumed that the national objective in any war was to break the enemy's will by offensive action, which would best be achieved by effecting the maximum destruction on the enemy's most vital objectives. The bombardment aircraft was the instrument for attaining this goal.

There were a number of other officers then at the Tactical School who were no less enthusiasts for the bomber. Lieutenant Kenneth L. Walker, an instructor for the Bombardment Section, was particularly active in the theory of offensive bombardment. Support and encouragement came from Major Donald Wilson who headed the Air Force Section which embraced strategic thinking. The ideas of the bomber advocates were well tested within the School in debate with other members of the faculty, notably those assigned to the Pursuit Section, at the time headed by Captain Claire L. Chennault* who had an almost fanatical obsession with the superiority of the fighter and was backed in most of his assertions by the pursuit tactics instructor Harold H. George.† Strangely two brother officers were ensconced in the Tactical School with names only differentiated by the middle initial,

* Claire Chennault commanded the American Volunteer Group in the China-Burma-India theatre early in World War II and later the 14th Air Force in China.
† Harold H. George commanded V Fighter Command in the early days of World War II.

although adherence to different points of view found them distinguished as 'Bomber George' and 'Fighter George'. The pursuit advocates insisted that the fighter by the nature of its design, would have ascendancy over the bomber through its speed and firepower, and that a well prepared fighter arm could defeat any bomber offensive. In terms of the lumbering Keystone bombers of 1932, easily overhauled by the Curtiss and Boeing pursuits* the fighter adherents had a strong case. But the technical advances of the early 1930s produced a changed situation.

In 1930 the Boeing Company of Seattle, Washington, produced a revolutionary transport aircraft employing new techniques in aluminium formers and skin. The designers discarded the traditional biplane layout, with its drag-producing struts and wires, for a single all-metal wing with integral strength obtained from cantilever construction. Moreover, further reductions in drag were obtained by fitting an hydraulic mechanism to retract the main wheels into the wing during flight. Although the Pratt and Whitney radial was only rated at 575 hp, it gave this aircraft a top speed as fast as the current Army pursuits.

Boeing saw an opening for a military version and proceeded to build a twin-engine aircraft incorporating the same engineering progress, although surrendering to tradition over the matter of crew accommodation in providing open cockpits. Not only was this advanced aircraft, designated YB-9, capable of a top speed close or equal to those of Army pursuits but it had built-in fuel tankage giving a radius of action over 260 miles with a ton of bombs. Budgetary restrictions limited purchase to seven machines for evaluation, but they provided the tacticians at Maxwell with the technical breakthrough to give credence to the ascendancy of the bombardment mission and likewise to influence many other Air Corps officers. In 1932 and 1933 the Bombardment Section had begun studying the percentage error of Air Corps' bombing practice and the various factors to be considered in achieving a high number of hits on a target. The types of target for strategic attack were also investigated. During this period the basic doctrine of strategic air operations was clarified, primarily a collective effort by the instructors and members of the Air Force and Bombardment Sections of the Tactical School although the prime architects were the respective principals of those departments, Major Donald Wilson and Captain Harold Lee George.

The Boeing YB-9 was soon eclipsed by a design from another company. Martin, whose GMB had been the first indigenous bomber in the Army's squadrons, had also made progress in the art of all-metal airframes. They produced a large twin-engine monoplane, roughly the same overall dimensions as the Keystones and the old NBS-1s. The prototype flew in July 1932 and, after re-working, underwent official tests at Wright Field in October as the Martin XB-10. Two of the new 675 horse-power Wright R-1820 radials and a reasonable degree of streamlining gave this aircraft the then astonishing top speed of over 200 mph, while range and payload were similar to the Boeing YB-9.

Another first for a U.S. warplane was the new Martin's primitive form of gun turret manually traversed; a glazed cupola was now a necessity to protect the nose gunner from the air blast at high speed. The pilot's and rear

* Boeing P-12 had a top speed of 171 mph against 121 mph for the Keystone LB-6A.

Martin B-12s of 31st BS, 7th BG, on the flight-line during manoeuvres. Nose turret of this then (1935) advanced aircraft was little more than a glassed cupola to protect gunner from the air blast. *R. Louden*

gunner's emplacements were also enclosed on the forty-eight production machines ordered in January 1933 and further purchases in 1935 and 1936 brought total orders to over 150 (including B-12 and B-14 variants). These bombers cost twice as much as the old Martin biplanes of 1920 ($50,840 apiece) reflecting both Government and War Department concern to modernise the Air Corps in the light of troubles in other continents.

Many production B-10s and variants were fitted with two-stage variable pitch propellers, recently perfected by Hamilton-Standard. Hydraulically actuated, the blades could be angled from low pitch for take-off to high for general flying. An in-flight variable pitch propeller had been long sought to maintain performance at high altitudes, particularly for aircraft with supercharged engines. Quickly following the introduction of the Hamilton-Standard propeller was renewed progress in turbo-supercharger experimentation. Installation of turbo-blowers was made to the R-1820 engines of a Martin B-10 (the YB-10A) in 1933. Flights reached over 30,000 feet and at 25,000 feet the optimum altitude for maximum performance, a speed of 236 mph was achieved. As yet, however, high altitude still played no great part in the concepts being formulated within the Air Corps, for the consuming interest was now that of range.

The Coastal Mission

The domains of the Army and Navy in defence of the United States had once been clearly defined by the bounds of land and water on the movement of their forces. Aircraft were not so restricted and those of the Navy could venture inland as easily as those of the Army could fly out to sea. The limits of this trespass were from the early post-war years the source of controversy between the two services. Aircraft were well suited to the task of coastal defence, which was vested in the Army, and the Air Service had hoped it might participate in this as a separate mission. The Navy jealously guarded its oceans and objected to any aerial encroachment by the Army. Not until January 1931 was the disagreement resolved, albeit temporarily, when verbal undertaking was reached by General Douglas MacArthur, then Army Chief of Staff, and Admiral William Platt, Chief of Naval Operations. Most notable outcome was the right of the Air Corps to engage in seaward flights of up to 100 miles in their task of coastal defence.

With oceanic coastlines extending to over 4,000 miles it was apparent that the range of existing Army bombers was quite inadequate to meet any seaborne invasion of the U.S.A., remote as such an event might be. There was also defence of the distant dependencies of Hawaii and the Philippines to be considered. With the less parochial diplomacy of the new Roosevelt administration, and sympathetic consideration of the War Department, this concession by the Navy was utilised by the Air Corps in July 1933 as reason for requesting manufacturers to produce a design study of a bomber with a radius of action of 2,500 miles. This gigantic step in view of previous range requirements resulted in the award of a contract to Boeing in June 1934 for preliminary design data for a very long-range aircraft, which would have four engines, stowage for 8,000 lb bombs and would gross 35 tons. A prototype was ordered the following year and development of an even bigger bomber by Douglas initiated. The Boeing, designated XB-15, completed in 1937, never went beyond the experimental stage, being rendered obsolete by the sheer pace of aeronautical technology. The sum of $609,300 expended on it would have been sufficient to purchase a complete squadron of B-10s.

While the Army General Staff had resisted all attempts by the Air Service/Air Corps to achieve autonomy, and was largely supported in this by the investigating boards that were periodically set up by Congress on various aspects, there is evidence that some of the hide-bound traditionalists within the Army upper echelons were not unmoved by the potential of air power. During the late 1920s the need for a self-contained air striking force with the necessary flexibility to operate both directly and indirectly in support of the ground forces and on special missions such as coastal protection, was being subscribed to in many quarters within the Army. This concept became known as the General Headquarters Air Force and the idea had gained enough favour by January 1933 for the War Department to authorise provisional formation under the then Assistant Chief of Air Corps, Brigadier General Oscar Westover.

To test out this concept an exercise was staged on the west coast where air units were concentrated to repel an imaginary seaborne invasion. The results not only endorsed the advantages of a General Headquarters Air Force, they also highlighted the superior performance of the new bombers in evading the participating pursuits. The 2nd Bombardment Group employed its few Boeing YB-9s with great success and this, plus testing of the new 200 mph Martin XB-10, prompted General Westover in his report to question the ability of pursuits to intercept effectively or safely even if they had the necessary speed to overhaul the bombers. His enthusiasm also led him to assert that the new bombers had such heavy firepower that, when flying in a close defensive formation, it appeared they could accomplish their mission without support. Westover underlined his beliefs with the maxim 'no known agency can frustrate the accomplishment of a bombardment mission.' All heady stuff, but reflecting the upsurge of Air Corps adherence

A lone prototype, the XB-15, provided both Boeing and 'Wright Field' with much valuable data on the design and operation of very large multi-engined aircraft.

Opposite:
The XB-15 landing at Langley Field, Virginia, while operated by the 96th BS, 2nd BG at that station. The four Wright R-1820 engines proved insufficiently powerful for this heavy aircraft.

to bomber dominance that the technical achievements of the B-9 and B-10 had brought.

On 1st March 1935, the General Headquarters Air Force was officially activated. Its position was in some respects ambiguous, in that it was wholly an Air Corps organisation, yet officially its commander, and that of the whole Air Corps, were on an equal footing under the Army General Staff. The important point was that air, not ground, officers controlled its operations. Brigadier General Frank Andrews was appointed Commander while Westover moved to Chief of the Air Corps.

A seemingly favourable financial climate found the Air Corps seeking bombers with better range and load even before the first Martin B-10s entered service. Early in 1934 they issued a new multi-engined bomber specification for interested manufacturers to compete with prototypes assessed at Wright Field. Martin produced an enlarged version of the B-10, Douglas a design based on their twin-engined transports, but Boeing's entry had four engines and as such was the first four-engine monoplane bomber offered to any air arm.

The Martin was the smallest of the three and though least expensive was eliminated because of limitations in payload. The Douglas could lift a maximum of 4,000 lb bombs and was able to fly 500 miles from base to deliver 2,200 lb at its cruising speed of 170 mph. The performance difference between the bulbous Douglas and the sleek Boeing made as striking a contrast as their appearance. The Boeing could haul the same weight of bombs double the distance at a cruising speed of over 200 mph. The only factor marring this major step in all-round performance was costs – the Boeing was double that of the Douglas.

The Air Corps, particularly impressed by the Boeing's performance which

could give them their first true long-range bomber, chose to order sixty-five Boeings when they could have had 185 Douglas aircraft. The War Department, having other ideas, allowed a contract for only thirteen test examples of the Boeing – to be designated YB-17* – while giving a major order to Douglas for 133 B-18s. Apparently War Department concern was that too generous a policy had been allowed to develop with the Air Corps, to the neglect of other branches of the Army which were badly in need of re-equipment. The Boeings, for which the company name was Flying Fortress, were delivered in 1937. Despite considerably better performance than the prototype their attributes did not bring further orders immediately, the War Department authorising expenditure on the less expensive shorter range Douglas B-18 series, a further 177 of which were procured in 1937 and another seventy-eight the following year.

There were other factors involved in this retrenchment by the War Department. Press coverage of the plight of Abyssinian civilians in Italian air raids, followed by the more sustained and graphic slaughter caused by bombing in China and Spain brought national condemnation and endeavours to strengthen America's policy of neutral isolationism. In this atmosphere the Army was sensitive to public feelings against aerial bombardment. Also the more conservative elements in the Army were again suspicious of Air Corps motives. Even if a general consciousness existed with the airmen to be more guarded over their ideals, any shrewd observer could gauge the overriding interest in strategic bombing objectives prevailing within the Air Corps.

There were also renewed rumblings from the quarter-deck, culminating in a strict 100 mile observance of seaward flights by the Air Corps in May 1938. This followed a top level protest by the Navy after a search for an interception of the *Rex* by three B-17s of the 2nd Bombardment Group when the Italian liner was 725 miles out from New York. The exercise, staged with an eye towards favourable publicity for the capabilities of long-range bombers in locating hostile fleets, backfired in that the Navy found it an unforgiveable encroachment upon their preserves.

In the same month further opposition to the long-range bomber was expressed by the U.S. Secretary of War in directing the Air Corps to limit its orders to only medium and attack (light) bombers in the fiscal year commencing June 1938. Faced with this edict, the Air Corps did some smart shifting of funds and managed to scrape together enough to place orders for thirty-nine B-17Bs in the current fiscal year, sufficient to establish a B-17 group on the west coast and complete that on the east.

The big XB-15, which flew for the first time in October 1937, would have no production order. Surprisingly the other giant long-range development, the Douglas XB-19, was not cancelled. Wright Field were able to insist that work on the prototype continue despite Douglas's willingness to abandon the project in the light of the current hostility towards the long-range bomber.

High-altitude Bombing

The first of the thirteen Boeing 'Flying Fortresses' had been delivered to the 2nd Bombardment Group at Langley Field in January 1937 and the last

* Actually designated Y1B-17 when delivered to signify funds used in their purchase.

24

arrived that August. These aircraft became the status symbol of the Air Corps as they represented the only four-engine all-metal monoplane bombers in service with any air force and their performance was certainly in advance of all contemporary bombers. Group commander was Colonel Robert Olds who had a long association with Army bombers and had once headed that section at the Tactical School. In view of the cost and sophistication of the cherished YB-17s, crews were hand picked – the Air Corps elite; they included Harold L. George, Curtis LeMay, Robert B. Williams, John Sanford, Niel Harding, Caleb Haynes, Archibald Y. Smith to name but a few who would become famous in World War II. The adverse publicity of a crash could not be afforded and hence great care was taken to see that only the experienced would fly and maintain the aircraft.

A fourteenth Flying Fortress had been built for experimental purposes and this, the YB-17A, was to be a test bed for another installation of turbo-superchargers. Experience with the turbo-supercharged PB-2A two-seat fighter and the YB-10A of the same era had shown the advantages of flight at high altitudes in achieving better speeds and fuel economy through the reduced airframe drag in lower density air. Superchargers were really viable when Hamilton-Standard and Curtiss Electric at last perfected their constant-speed propellers in 1935. A governor in the hub automatically adjusted blade pitch as air density varied. Hamilton-Standard followed this, in 1938, with a fully-feathering propeller giving a valuable safety factor in that blades could be angled to prevent windmilling and dangerous vibration in the event of engine failure.

The YB-17A, first flown in April 1938, was plagued with serious vibration when the superchargers were turned on. The trouble, traced to their positioning and necessitating re-siting, caused delays until the end of the year. In subsequent flights from Wright Field the YB-17A improved the Flying

Pride of the Air Corps during the late 'thirties, the YB-17s of 2nd BG were then the most advanced multi-engine aircraft in the world. Their combat capability was questionable despite the famous tag 'Flying Fortress'.

Fortresses' ceiling by an extra 9,000 feet and increased top speed by 30 mph at 25,000 feet. The advantage of equipping future bombers with turbo superchargers was evident and the B-17B, then in production, featured these as standard equipment.

Attack from high altitudes offered the bomber a better chance of reaching objectives. Air Corps planners believed that fighters would have great difficulty in reaching high-flying bombers before they were out of range. The accuracy of anti-aircraft ground artillery also declined as altitudes rose. Accurate bombing from great heights would be necessary but this seemed feasible as the Norden bomb sight had already proved extremely accurate in a number of trials from medium altitudes. In 1935, the 19th Bombardment Group, located at Rockwell Field, California, had conducted a six-week bombing programme on the range at Muroc Dry Lake, sighting with Nordens in its Martin B-10 and B-12s from 15,000 feet. At the end of this period the average error for the Group's bombardiers was only 164 feet from the aiming point. With the B-17, a much more stable aircraft, similarly good results were obtained in 1938 and 1939.

Thus the B-17 offered a combination of range, speed, high altitude and accurate bombing, meeting the immediate Air Corps quest for a bomber to fill an offensive role. But at this juncture – 1938 – elements within the Army General Staff and War Department would still not condone attempts to establish a strategic bombing force. Their actions to suppress these Air Corps endeavours were sadly out of line with the new outlook of President Roosevelt who, as early as January 1938, had commented on the 'warlike preparations abroad' and the threat to world peace, heralding a radical change in U.S. foreign policy. The President's first move was to rejuvenate the Navy by an injection of funds much needed for new ships and modern carrier-based aircraft. He then indicated his intention of asking Congress for funds for a vast expansion of the Air Corps, a sum which when passed early in April 1939 allowed the Air Corps to order 3,251 new aircraft – double the number in hand at the time. National defence now embraced 'the whole western hemisphere' which included the Caribbean and the approaches to Canada and South America. Long-ranged aircraft were imperative to meet this situation and those who had so recently been intent on stifling this type of aircraft were forced to think again. Even so in some quarters War Department and General Staff opposition to the bomber still persisted and the displeasure at the activities of the commander and deputy of GHQ Air Force, Brigadier General Frank Andrews and Colonel Hugh Kneer, resulted in positions of demotion when their terms expired in the spring of 1939.

General Westover had been killed in an accident in September 1938 and his place was taken by his assistant, Major General Henry 'Hap' Arnold. Arnold was another officer believing in the strategic bomber as the paramount air weapon and he pursued the cause with no less vigour than his predecessors. Among his immediate goals were more B-17s to fulfil the needs of hemisphere defence, a requirement the War Department could no longer deny on any basis.

Deliveries of the first true production models of the Flying Fortress, the B-17B, for which the Air Corps had scraped the bottom of their appropriations barrel, commenced in October 1939. Unfortunately trouble was experienced with turbo-superchargers seizing and disintegrating, and the

necessary modifications to improve lubrication held up deliveries, so that it was March 1940 before the last B-17B reached the Air Corps. These bombers were shared between the 2nd and 7th Bombardment Group meeting the plan to establish a B-17 group on each coast. The B-17B gave practical application to the theories of high-altitude precision bombing which had been evolved within GHQ Air Force, whose personnel were well primed with the doctrine taught at the Air Corps Tactical School. During 1940 the 2nd and 7th Groups practised high-altitude attack over bombing ranges with increasing success, and by the end of that year bombardiers were sighting from 20,000 feet with frequent strikes on the target. Targets usually took the form of brightly marked circles of two and four hundred feet diameter. In the centre of the inner circle was a small shed used to store marking materials, so situated because it was at one time reasoned to be the safest place! The Norden sight and a proficient bombardier removed this sanctuary and with the B-17 it was not uncommon to hit the shack – from whence arose the term 'shacked' meaning dead on target. Such accuracy led to inflated comments of 'pickle barrel' bombing that would be something of an embarrassment in view of later happenings. The important factor overlooked by those who enthused about results is that they were obtained in near ideal conditions of excellent visibility. Few parts of the globe provided the arid clear conditions that were usually found over Muroc Dry Lake.

The General Electric turbo-supercharger turbine assembly as fitted to the B-17.

Bomber Defences

Despite the fact that the performance of fighters had been improved to a point where they were some 60 mph faster than the speediest bombers, the adherence to the doctrine of daylight bombardment was not diminished. High performance fighters dominated the European air war and even in the U.S.A. the Lockheed P-38 fighter ordered for the Army had a top speed in excess of 400 mph and sufficient range and heavy armament to make it an excellent bomber destroyer. Neither had the promoters of the long-range bomber in the early 'thirties visualised the successful development of radio wave location and the radar warning systems that in 1940 proved decisive in the defence of Britain against air attack. Both British and German experience with day bombers during the battles of western Europe in the same year was clearly that bombers could not operate in daylight without prohibitive losses at the hands of opposing fighters. The bombers involved – Blenheim, Dornier 17, Junkers 88, Wellington, Heinkel 111 – were all of medium or light classification and their operational speeds were as fast or faster than that of the B-17B. The U.S. had Air Corps observers in England and were aware of these facts but even so it appears to have had little effect upon the Air Corps' adherence to daylight bombardment. If anything the experience of the Luftwaffe and Royal Air Force hardened opinion among Air Corps tacticians that high-altitude attack in mass defensive formation was a highly credible method of reaching a target with minimum loss. The protection afforded a formation by the combined firepower of flexible machine-guns on each aircraft had been seen in World War I day bombing raids. Since then formation flying to and from the target had been the standard tactic for Air Corps day bombers, with multiples of the three-plane vee-positioned flight making up a nine or twelve-plane squadron formation.

The five defensive positions of the B-17 had been considered formidable in 1935 – and in fact brought about the popular name Flying Fortress. The Air Corps tended to assume adversaries would have similar capabilities to their own pursuits and the armament of early B-17s was probably quite adequate to fight off such aircraft – if intercepted. The superior speeds of the B-17 gave it ability to evade interception. Hence their defensive armament was not improved to any great degree, although Wright Field had pointed out deficiencies at an early date. When, in 1938, the RAF's Air Marshal Arthur Harris was sent on an evaluation visit to the U.S. aircraft industry his report on the armament of the YB-17s he inspected was damning to the point of opinion that the aircraft was quite incapable of defending itself from attack by modern interceptors. The original specification of the B-17 had called for four 0.50 calibre machine guns which had twice the effective range (1,000 yards maximum) of the rifle calibre 0.30 types standard in most air forces, but the five guns on the YB-17s were 0.30s until 1940.

The 0.50 inch calibre gun was designed late in World War I and adopted as the 'heavy' machine-gun for U.S. Army aircraft in 1922. Although many pursuits, attack and bomber types had this weapon specified, during the following eighteen years they were often omitted or had 0.30 models in lieu. The reason was primarily one of cost, there being an ample supply of 0.30 guns. The acquisition of the larger 'point fifties', basically scaled up versions of the former, was on such a limited scale that insufficient were available for arming even the vaunted Flying Fortress. The inadequacy of

A smooth 'in train' release of ten practice bombs from a B-17C. The accuracy that could be achieved with the Norden in the stable B-17 led to the gross press exaggeration that it was possible to drop bombs into a pickle barrel from three miles high.

Opposite:
The second giant bomber prototype ordered by the Air Corps took nearly five years to complete and cost over five million dollars. Making its first flight in June 1941, the Douglas XB-19 was the first aircraft to use the 2,000 horse-power rated Wright R-3350 radials, later versions of which powered the B-29.

B-17 armament was highlighted by the power turrets on European bombers and steps were taken to instal the larger Browning in all four gunner-manned posts on the B-17B. Improvement of fields of fire from the dorsal and side positions was achieved by removing the enclosing 'blister' structures, and for ventral defence a more practical gunners' 'bathtub' was provided, Although the Sperry Company began work early in 1940 on a manned upper turret and a periscope-sighted lower turret for the B-17, development and production problems took some eighteen months to overcome.

A New Bomber

Whatever the deficiencies of the B-17 it was the only aircraft that could immediately meet the requirement of hemisphere defence and a strategic

bombing mission if the United States should become involved in war. Early in 1939 General Arnold was seeking another manufacturer to expand B-17 production rapidly if necessary. Consolidated Aircraft Corporation of San Diego, California, was approached in view of their experience in building large multi-engined seaplanes. The reaction, reflecting company pride, was to offer to design a new bomber rather than licence-build one already five years old. With Consolidated's assurance that this could be achieved with minimum delay by utilising the wing, engine and tail components already in being for an advanced seaplane, the Air Corps gave the go-ahead for a design study, following this with an order for a prototype and test examples after the expansion programme was approved by Congress in April 1939.

The prototype of the new bomber, the XB-24, first flew in December

1939 and subsequent flights confirmed that it had all-round performance advantages over the B-17. The Air Corps, however, was backing both types, by the spring of 1940 it had on order thirty-eight B-24s and another thirty-eight B-17s. Much larger orders were to follow.

Even larger bombers, with double the range of the B-17 and B-24, were being sought to meet ostensibly the needs of hemisphere defence. In November 1939 General Arnold obtained War Department permission to proceed with design proposals for such an aircraft. In fact, the range and bombload requirements issued to manufacturers in January 1940 were not dissimilar to those that resulted in the old XB-15. Four proposals from industry each received a contract in June 1940 for preliminary data, although two designs were withdrawn soon after, leaving the Boeing XB-29 and Consolidated XB-32. The former was the preferred design, but contracts for prototypes from both firms ensued in September, in furtherance of a policy of having a back-up design in case one should be fraught with development problems. Both bombers were to use the new 2,200 horse-power Wright R-3350 radial engine to give a 2,000 mile radius of action, but the Boeing XB-29 was to carry a substantially greater bombload of 16,000 lb over this distance, double that of the XB-32.

These orders reflected the remarkable change in Air Corps fortunes, when only two years before a meagre order for more B-17s had been denied. During the expansion period from 1939 all types of new military aircraft were being developed and ordered, but the Air Corps was undoubtedly still mainly concerned with bombers. When the Nazi armies swept through western Europe in the spring of 1940 they did so with the decisive support of the Luftwaffe. Confronted with this indisputable evidence of the vital role of air power in a modern conflict, opposition within the U.S. Government and the War Department to the Air Corps' insatiable requirements melted away.

As related, the basic precedents of strategic bombardment stemmed from World War I. The progress made by United States' manufacturers and official establishments in aeronautical technology produced the equipment, weapons and aircraft that during the course of the 1930s focused attention upon high-altitude precision attack as the favoured means of conducting strategic bombardment. Of the world's air forces engulfed, or about to be so, in World War II the USAAC was the only one with this precise doctrine and capability. To a great extent this had been promoted as the key to autonomy, that was still denied.

2. Early War Plans and Preparations

By mid-autumn 1940 most military leaders in the United States believed that it was only a matter of time before their country would be at war with the Axis powers – Japan having allied herself with Germany and Italy in September that year. American sympathy and support tended towards Britain to where an enormous quantity of weapons and equipment was being supplied, particularly aircraft, To aid her own re-armament programme, America sought technical and tactical information from Britain and a measure of co-operation was gradually built up on military matters. Although the United States still pronounced a neutral line her leaders were active in their condemnation of the belligerent activities of Germany and plans were made for the eventuality of war. For this reason it was deemed expedient to establish a measure of collaboration with the British and in late January 1941 formal military staff discussions commenced in Washington.

The results of the American-British exchanges were incorporated in a document covering grand strategy, and known as ABC 1. It dealt with the way by which the United States and British Commonwealth might defeat Germany and the Axis powers *if* the United States became embroiled. As Germany was the strongest Axis member it was considered that its defeat should be given first priority, while containing actions were fought in the Pacific if it became necessary to be involved in hostilities with Japan.

To defeat Germany, a 'sustained air offensive against German military power' and the desire to see 'U.S. Army air bombardment units operate offensively in collaboration with the Royal Air Force' was written into the document. The British had advised that it would be impossible to re-establish an army on the continent before the German war machine had been substantially weakened, and to this end they were already building a large force of heavy bombers for strategic assault. At this time the British could speak from bitter experience – and their influence weighed heavily in the discussions culminating in ABC-1. While this document only represented a broad outline of mutual policy to be followed *if* America entered the war, it had in effect the War Department's tacit approval to plans for strategic bombing. Furthermore, the implications of ABC-1 were incorporated in a joint U.S. Army-Navy plan (RAINBOW 5) without apparent dissent on the reference to a bombing offensive. For the first time there were signs of a general acceptance of offensive air power by the traditional military establishment.

The tentative war plans prompted many problems, not least the massive production programme that would be required to meet a war situation. In

July 1941 President Roosevelt asked the Secretaries of War and of the Navy to provide an estimate of the overall production requirements necessary to defeat the potential enemies. General Arnold took the opportunity of seeking permission for the Army Air Forces (AAF)* to prepare their own report, instead of through the War Plans Division of the War Department, ostensibly to alleviate the workload of that Division, hard pressed to complete the complex study of ground force requirements to meet the President's short deadline date. Arnold pointed out that the AAF's own Air War Plans Division was well suited to this task. The request was conceded, perhaps because at that date – August 4th – only a week remained to complete the whole report. So far as the AAF leaders were concerned, this now allowed them to formulate their requirements without interference from ground-war orientated officers.

The Air War Plans Division was only a few weeks old, having been set up by Arnold to develop comprehensive plans for AAF activities. The staff officers, if junior in rank, were both experienced and talented. The Division Chief was Colonel Harold L. George, his deputy Lieutenant Colonel Kenneth Walker, the same men who, as directors of the Bombardment Section at the Tactical School a decade earlier, had played an important part in the promotion of strategic bombardment as the Air Corps' article of faith.

The third member of the Division, Major Haywood Hansell, had also served as an instructor in the Bombardment Section at Maxwell and more recently had been a prime mover in forming an intelligence section for the AAF. He also arranged for suitable material, notably from Britain from where he had just returned. To aid preparation of the report a fourth officer joined the team, Major Laurence S. Kuter, yet another former Bombardment Instructor at the Tactical School.

The document they produced (AWPD/1) was remarkable for its perception and thoroughness. To justify the production requirements a detailed plan of utilisation was made out. The authors were well aware of past opposition by the War Department to strategic bombing and while AAF involvement in such a campaign had in effect been sanctioned in the recent ABC-1 agreement with the British, and endorsed in RAINBOW 5, there was no guarantee that the Army leadership might not have second thoughts. The draft was cleverly constructed following the guidelines of the policy documents so that the War Department and General Staff were denied political reasons for objecting. While covering all aspects of AAF requirements it was to be expected, in the light of the authors' backgrounds, that the assault on Germany would be a particularly precise and carefully prepared study.

AWPD/1 detailed three main tasks: air operations in defence of the Western Hemisphere, an unremitting air offensive against Germany and assistance in strategic defence in the Pacific. In the case of Germany, if

---

* The new overall title for the air arm introduced in June 1941. The Air Corps and Air Force Combat Command (new name for GHQ Air Force) remained in being until 9th March 1942 when both disappeared as a result of a further reorganisation which gave the AAF semi-autonomy. At this time it was co-equal with the Army Ground and Service forces under the Chief of Staff.

an invasion was later necessary then full air support would be provided for the forces involved, but the implication was that strategic bombing might make a land campaign unnecessary. If Japan entered the war, it was to be subjected to an aerial assault after Germany had been defeated.

The plan enumerated types of target to be attacked in bringing about a breakdown of Germany's industrial and economic structure. First priority was the electric power grid, one of the most extensive in the world, on which most of German war industry was highly dependent. Second target system was the transportation networks: rail, road and canals. Third was the oil and petroleum industry, particularly the synthetic manufacturing plants. An intermediate objective and necessary prerequisite to the attack on these priority targets was neutralisation of the German Air Force through attacks on bases, aircraft and associated manufacturing plants. It might also be necessary to attack submarine and naval facilities to protect friendly shipping and ensure supply routes. Bombing of targets with civilian connections would only be undertaken when German morale was breaking.

AWPD/1 even went as far as listing 154 targets, the elimination of which was deemed necessary to bring about the desired demise of German war industry. A time schedule for their destruction, based on bombing error factors, the number of sorties required, weather obstacles, enemy defences, attrition plus the precise numbers and types of aircraft involved was included. The objectives would primarily be achieved by a force of 1,360 B-17s and B-24s (20 groups) based in England and 816 B-29s and B-32s (12 groups) based in Northern Ireland. In southern England 850 B-25 and B-26 medium bombers (ten groups) would support the campaign but range limitations would keep them from most strategic targets. Base defence and limited escort for this force rested primarily on 1,300 fighters (ten groups) also based in southern England. It was further planned to set up bases in the Cairo area for another 816 B-29s (twelve groups) with 780 fighters (six groups) for base area defence. All told, the estimate ran to 3,842 bombers with another 1,288 as replacements for losses. Fighters totalled 2,080 plus 335 replacements. There were also plans to use very long range bombers with 4,000 mile radius of action which could operate from bases in Newfoundland, Greenland, Africa or India. Designs of this nature were currently being investigated, a significant reason being the possibility that Britain might fall to the Germans and the AAF be denied the bases essential for the use of B-17, B-24 and B-29 types.

Time schedule for this massive operation from the outbreak of war was, one year for production, nine months for deployment and six months to achieve the desired results. Overall aircraft numbers set out in AWPD/1, to meet operations in the Western Hemisphere, Europe and in the Pacific were, including trainers and reserves, a prodigious 68,416. Manpower requirements, both flying and non-flying personnel amounted to 2,164,916.

The four officers preparing the plan completed their task in seven days of unabated activity. The document went far beyond the original Presidential request, but its very comprehensiveness undoubtedly enhanced chances of acceptance. There followed the delicate job of presenting AWPD/1 for approval. The method agreed was for the four authors to give explanatory introductory sessions – with the aid of maps and diagrams – to selected audiences. They began with those members of the War Department and

General Staff who were more likely to be sympathetic to their ideas and, finding success, went on to receive a favourable audience with General Marshall, the Army Chief of Staff.

Colonel George and his team sagely emphasised that Army planners had stated it would take two years to train, assemble and deploy the necessary ground forces to conduct a land campaign in Europe, while the AAF could begin operations within a year. There was also the necessity of ensuring Allied air superiority before any invasion could be staged, so that an air assault on Germany was an essential prerequisite. Consequently the Army had at last approved a plan which boldly dictated an independent mission for its airmen – one sought for over twenty years. AWPD/1 still had to pass before the Army-Navy Joint Board, set up to consider the overall production assessment for the President, where it seemed highly improbable the Navy element would give it free passage. However General Marshall, for reasons on which one can only speculate, chose to bypass the Joint Board and send AWPD/1 direct to the Secretary of War, Henry Stimson. The plan was accepted as the broad basis of AAF war doctrine and came to be accepted as such by the U.S. Government.

The Japanese attack on Pearl Harbour on 7th December 1941 brought the United States into hostilities with a nasty jolt; the U.S. Navy was then too occupied with its smarting wounds and the contingencies of war at sea to interfere in the ambitious plan of the Army Air Forces. With further endorsement of the AAF's general line of strategy at a meeting between the American and British chiefs early in 1942, the way was open for action towards the physical realisation of the bombing force required. There were to be complications. Serious situations developing in other combat theatres caused the diversion of bomber units earmarked for the United Kingdom. The various Allied plans for an early invasion in Western Europe to take pressure off the Russian front, resulting in the North African landings of November 1942, brought further delays and changes in the composition of the forces being assembled. Despite these deviations, a strategic bomber offensive against Germany remained the principal AAF goal.

Building the Bomber Force

First priorities were vast expansion of aircraft production and associated equipment. Precedence was given to the manufacture of heavy bombers needed immediately for defensive operations in the Pacific and anti-submarine patrols, apart from the proposed strategic bombing of Germany. In January 1942 a target of 11,300 medium and heavy bombers for the year was set, including 1,520 allocated to the Navy for patrol purposes, and 2,333 off-set to the British. By the following year it was hoped to raise medium and heavy bomber production to some 3,000 units per month for an annual total of 32,000, of which 3,810 were for the Navy. These targets proved too ambitious and others set were to be varied in turn by events overtaking policies.

The actual production of medium and heavy bombers achieved in 1942 was 6,553, with 683 going to the Navy and 1,200 to other countries, mainly Britain and Russia. For 1943 total heavy and medium bomber production was 16,830, the AAF receiving 12,684.

The assault on Germany, as planned in AWPD/1, depended on B-17, B-24, B-29 and B-32 aircraft. Prototypes of the latter two were still under construcion and production examples many months away. The B-17 and B-24 were therefore an immediate requirement, but in January 1942 the two plants producing them were only averaging three a day, a far cry from the projected flow. Fortuitously, extensive measures had already been taken to expand the U.S. aircraft and aero products industry. In the immediate pre-war years the British and French had shopped for aircraft and had given the industry a welcome stimulus. With the war in Europe, most American aircraft firms had more foreign orders than they could comfortably meet. In 1940 the position for Air Corps orders had not been lack of funds, but the inability of manufacturers to accept the additional work. General Arnold's staff, assessing this situation earlier, had advocated new manufacturing plants. Financial approval during the latter half of 1940 led to arrangements for a score of new airframe and aero engine plants which, fortunately, proved to have a capacity well beyond the production levels envisaged at that time.

To build and tool plants takes some two years, but the task had been initiated eighteen months before America entered the war. But even at full production capacity, the Seattle and San Diego plants of Boeing and Consolidated could not hope to provide sufficient heavy bombers to meet AAF requirements, so alternative sources of production were sought. The manufacture of B-17s under licence was arranged with Lockheed-Vega at Burbank, and Douglas at Long Beach, both in California. The two plants started producing the bombers during 1942, although some months were needed to reach full production.

Demand for the B-24 Liberator, also required by the U.S. Navy and Britain for maritime patrol and anti-submarine work, was greater than the San Diego plant could supply. The Ford Motor Company were appointed to make knock-down B-24 sections on a mass production basis and supply these to new assembly plants at Fort Worth, Texas (Consolidated), and Tulsa, Oklahoma (Douglas). Such was the capacity of the giant Ford plant at Willow Run, Michigan, that it was later agreed Ford would also open an assembly line at this site. A fifth source of B-24 production was arranged with North American for their Dallas, Texas, factory. The new plants took until late 1943 to get into full swing, but by early 1944 B-24s were being completed at almost double the rate of B-17s.

Production targets tended to be optimistic and subject to frequent revision. From the average three heavy bombers a day leaving the factories in January 1942 the figure jumped to twelve by the end of that year and doubled six months later. Peak production of B-17s and B-24s eventually, in March 1944, reached fifty a day. This coincided with the formation and despatch of the last heavy bomber units with these types to combat zones.

Similar plans were made for the new B-29, classified as a very heavy bomber; four plants were programmed to manufacture it in quantity long before the prototype flew in September 1942. Increased production had also been arranged for ordnance and a wide variety of materials necessary to equip and maintain combat units. More than 15,000 factories were involved in the contribution to the overall air force programme by 1944.

The basic flying unit of the AAF, like that of the RAF, was the squadron. The composition of a squadron varied, dependent on its designated mission, which was incorporated in all unit titles from 1923. At the time of Pearl Harbour the current aircraft establishment of a heavy bomber squadron was eight, whereas that for medium and light bombers was thirteen, and fighters twenty-five. Combat squadrons were usually organised into groups, a bomber group normally having four and a fighter group three; squadrons usually remained a permanent part of their parent group. For some years the Army had tended to use the group, rather than the squadron, as the basic tactical formation; this concept giving the most operationally viable, and economically supported combat unit.

A heavy bombardment group establishment was thirty-five aircraft, including three for use of the group headquarters. During 1942 all a group's aircraft were assigned to component squadrons; eight continued to be the authorised aircraft establishment, but usually a ninth machine was assigned to each squadron for use as a 'staff ship'. The intention of raising the authorised complement of a bombardment group by the equivalent of another squadron during 1944, was a point made in AWPD/1. This was actually effected late in 1943 when each squadron establishment was brought to a strength of fourteen, two of which were considered reserves.

The twenty-four groups that the Air Corps had planned in April 1939 was revised to forty-one groups in May 1940, only to be changed to fifty-four two months later, then to eighty-four in October 1941, 115 in January 1942, 224 in the following July and 273 in September that year. Of the last figure, to be attained by the end of December 1943, more than half were bomber groups with the largest single type being heavy bombardment. The actual number achieved by this date was 270 activated groups, 104 being heavy or very heavy bomber: this was the point of peak strength. Many of these groups were, however, only partly manned and equipped and in a few cases were a nucleus of men. In December 1941 the Air Corps had seventy activated groups on paper, fourteen being heavy bombardment groups but only three of those were fully equipped with B-17s, there then being only 157 B-17s and B-24s in the service.

The 384,535 men in the AAF when war began was a far cry from two million needed, but training facilities were good and well suited to meet the influx of personnel. The Air Corps had arranged for primary training through civilian contractors in 1939 and by the time the U.S. went to war forty-one such centres were in use. At this time the AAF was turning out 37,000 pilots annually and 110,000 specialised air and ground operatives. Where heavy bomber training was concerned the primary need was more aircraft, a shortage that during the first year of war was the cause of many personnel being posted to operational units without sufficient familiarisation with the types they were to operate.

3. Operations: Against Germany

A meeting of American and British leaders in January 1942 endorsed decisions to concentrate a combined war effort first against Nazi Germany. But the humiliation of the Japanese blow at Pearl Harbour and the other defeats in the Pacific were of more immediate concern to the American people. While the United States Government did not deviate from the war plan, there was need of a few flag waving feats against the Japanese to lift public morale. The bombing raid on Tokyo in April by Colonel James Doolittle's B-25s launched from a carrier, filled the bill in all respects.

Another force was also prepared to hit Japan from the air with B-24 Liberators using bases in China. Two dozen Liberators, appropriated from a consignment built for Britain, were manned by some of the first American crews trained to handle this comparatively new bomber. Colonel Harry Halverson commanded this task force, which had no formal designation, an unofficial tag being Halverson Detachment while the project was secretly planned under the code name HALPRO. With Japanese domination of Burma and the Dutch East Indies the route to China now lay via Africa and India. The Halverson detachment left the United States in May, flew the South Atlantic and had got as far as Khartoum where it was held, pending a decision on its final destination, as a Japanese offensive in China was threatening the proposed bases.

At this juncture a high level decision was made to use this small force in a gesture of assistance to the Soviets by bombing the Ploesti oil refineries. From this Rumanian complex the Germans drew most of the fuel for their Russian campaign, and in fact 25 per cent of their total petroleum products. To reach Ploesti, over a thousand miles from Egypt, the B-24s would have to carry extra fuel tanks in their bays, thereby restricting the bomb load. To conserve fuel reserves, Halverson elected to violate Turkish air space and to make good the escape from hostile territory by returning to Ramadi in Iraq rather than Egypt. With extra fuel and 3,000 lb of bombs each, thirteen B-24Ds led by Halverson took off late in the evening of 11th June. Flying singly through the night the bombers arrived over Rumania at dawn to find much of the country screened by cloud. Ten eventually located the Ploesti area, but their bombs apparently caused little damage; the other three unloaded over targets of opportunity. The enemy, evidently caught off guard by the raid, offered little opposition but unfortunately imprecise navigation and other factors caused some Liberators to lose their way or become dangerously low on fuel. As a result only seven aircraft reached Iraq; one crash landed, while two landed in Syria and four in Turkey where the crews were interned. In the naïve hope the Germans might not recognise the true objective, there was no Allied announcement of the mission, and only obscure references to American bombers getting off course while flying to Russia were made in the world's press. The Germans, however, were in no doubts as to the objectives. If this mission was a failure and costly in precious bombers – no airmen were killed – it was nonetheless historic for being the first operation of any kind undertaken by the AAF in Europe; it was also the first planned AAF strategic bombing of the war.

The remnants of Halverson Detachment never moved on to China for the Middle East situation had become so critical that there was a possibility the Germans might take Egypt and every bomber was needed to avert this. The Halverson Liberators were soon joined with a few B-17Es flown up from India to form the 1st Provisional Group. In addition the first complete B-24 group despatched from the United States, the 98th, went to the Middle East and in August joined the 1st Provisional Group in operations supporting ground and sea forces, chiefly raids against ports and shipping.

Establishment of the Eighth Air Force

The first lone strategic mission undertaken by AAF bombers was occasioned more by political expediency than military strategy. Despite the course of the war, the AAF's leaders had the creation and basing of a huge bomber force in the United Kingdom as a major aim and, at the time of the Ploesti raid, the first units were preparing for transatlantic movement.

In April 1941 a United States military mission, known as the Army Special Observer Group, was established in London under the command of Major General James E. Chaney; its purpose being preparation for possible involvement of United States ground and air forces in the European conflict. With that event, this group became the United States Army Forces in British Isles and accelerated its work. With Allied leaders agreed on the build-up of an expeditionary force in the United Kingdom for a proposed invasion of continental Europe in the autumn of 1942, or spring the following year, the AAF lost no time in making the initial moves towards setting up a heavy bomber command in England.

Arnold chose an old colleague, Major General Carl Spaatz, then head of Air Force Combat Command, to supervise the preparations and eventually to assume command of the whole AAF effort in the United Kingdom. To head the bomber command Arnold selected Brigadier General Ira Eaker, whose natural diplomacy would be an asset in negotiations with the British, on whom there would be an initial dependence in many spheres. Eaker and his staff of six arrived in England on 20th February 1942 and two days later the U.S. Army Bomber Command was formed under Chaney's forces. The newcomers were soon installed at RAF Bomber Command Headquarters to understudy procedures, establish liaison, and plan in detail the many factors involved in establishing the bomber force.

General Arnold wished to see air force control placed in a command structure between Eaker's Bomber Command and Chaney's Theatre Command, to give the American air arm a status on a par with the Royal Air Force in the Allied establishment. Chaney's staff, principally ground officers, saw no need for this, but Arnold persisted and eventually had his way. Designated the Eighth Air Force (8th AF), the new command was

B-17F Fortress of 8th AF's 305th BG.

B-24D Liberator of 8th AF's 44th BG.

officially secured in England with the arrival of Spaatz on 18th June 1942. The 8th AF had been formed in January 1942 to conduct operations in support of a proposed Allied invasion of North-West Africa later that year, only to find itself without a task when this plan was abandoned the following month. Spaatz then took over 8th AF as a headquarters for his project. Here too the 8th AF was basically committed to supporting an invasion and the combat groups that were assigned – and then frequently re-assigned elsewhere – embraced fighting, observation, photographic, troop carrying, light and medium bombardment as well as heavy bombardment roles. In April there were forty-nine groups earmarked, including twenty-three heavy bomb groups: by the end of June a force of sixty groups was scheduled but only seventeen were heavy bomber and the pressing needs of the other theatres of war caused further inroads into the heavy bomber units as plans were further amended. Despite the accelerated programme for opening a 'Second Front' to take pressure from the hard-pressed Russians, the AAF still intended to take any opportunity to engage its B-17s and B-24s in strategic bombardment. In this, the 8th AF were in congenial company, for RAF Bomber Command was equally dedicated to this aim.

The concept of strategic bombing as explored in 1918 had been sustained by the RAF throughout the inter-war years although, in contrast to the Air Corps development, bomber designs tended to be neglected compared to that of fighters. The British advocated night operations for their long-range bombers to minimise losses and the new four-engine heavy bombers in large-scale production in 1942 were, from the outset, designed for night attack. Approximating in size to the B-17 and B-24, the most notable difference was the much greater payload of the British machines, a normal 14,000 lb of bombs as against 4,000 lb. The bays of the Stirling, Halifax and Lancaster could accommodate very much larger weapons, whereas a 2,000 lb bomb was the maximum size that could be placed in the B-17 or B-24. In the B-17's case this stemmed from the design requirement for a *medium* bomber. Boeing, while keeping to the bomb load specified, provided exceptional endurance and four engines. In effect, the B-17 had a medium bomber payload with heavy bomber delivery capability. Although the B-24 was initiated nearly five years later than the B-17, it was designed for bombs of 2,000 lb maximum size, because the Air Corps interest in precision bombardment favoured quantity, so that the number of bombs released increased the number of strikes. The Liberator did, however, have accommodation for an 8,000 lb maximum load, but other factors often limited the operational load to half the maximum, basically through high wing loading and aerodynamic problems at high altitudes.

The RAF were understandably critical of the uneconomic prospect of the U.S. bombers, which had crews of ten and two-ton bomb loads compared with crews of seven and seven-ton bomb loads of their own heavies. The Americans stressed that their form of attack rested on accuracy, and that one 1,000-pounder on the target was of greater value than a dozen four-thousand pounders scattered around the target area, as might be the case in the RAF's night assaults which relied on chance and the weight of attack to destroy a small target. The RAF were encouraged in their scepticism of the American intentions by their own experiences of high-altitude bombing with the Fortress during the previous summer.

In 1940 the purchase of twenty B-17Cs by the RAF had been arranged not without political motivation, both British and U.S. Governments seeing the combat use of the most publicised American combat aircraft as a good advertisement – but for different reasons. The Air Corps were not happy about the transaction; they knew the RAF to be critical of B-17 defensive armament, and they were anxious to avoid any adverse publicity of the aircraft or its role that could be exploited by opponents at home. Also, they were short of B-17s. On the other hand RAF Bomber Command had already experienced heavy losses in daylight raids and was not enthusiastic. However, the stratospheric capability of the B-17 did offer an unexplored method of operation and the RAF sought to use these aircraft at altitudes of between thirty and 35,000 feet – some ten thousand feet above those used by the AAF –

which enemy interceptors might have great difficulty in reaching. In the event, the strain of continued operations at these great heights on both crews and aircraft brought many problems proving the venture impracticable. Although German fighters did make a few successful interceptions they took place only when the Fortresses were forced by malfunction or crew difficulties to lower altitudes.

British experience with the B-17Cs must have agitated and irritated the AAF bomber enthusiasts, but it did not deter them. The RAF had negligible success in bombing due to the excessive height of attack, and their bomb sights lacked the precision and sophistication of the Norden – withheld for fear it might prematurely fall into enemy hands. With their Norden, used from the optimum altitude of 25,000 feet, the AAF was confident of bombing accuracy. Nevertheless, the bomber still had to get safely to the target and the tactics planned were developed before radar warning systems came into widespread use, removing the advantage of surprise. Speed no longer offered an escape from interception, as the latest German fighters could easily overhaul a laden Fortress. Height would give some measure of diminishing the accuracy of anti-aircraft ground fire.

The AAF placed reliance on the ability of their bombers to fight their way through to the target, a costly tactic in RAF experience, for which they thought the Fortress no better suited than any other large bomber type. The AAF could point out that the RAF never flew their few Fortresses in large defensive formations – their operations were, perforce, by single aircraft or never more than four – and that the new B-17E model, coming into service late in 1942, had superior armament, making it the most heavily defended bomber in the world. The RAF warned that the American observers had under-estimated the capabilities of the Luftwaffe day fighter and encouraged Spaatz to concentrate on night operations, even if the B-17 and B-24 were not ideal for the purpose. Nonetheless, the RAF gave unstinted assistance to help the 8th AF prepare to test their daylight concept.

Arrangements were made for American aircrews to receive training on navigational, flying control and communications systems in use in the U.K. The 8th AF also planned its own training facilities. Air and ordnance depots were secured from the British and arrangements were made to take over airfields, eventually totalling 127, 75 of which would be prepared for bombers. After considering the area around York, offering the nearest extensive airfield locality to the major ports at Liverpool and the Clyde, where men and materials would arrive, the choice finally fell on the greater East Anglian area, a relatively flat plain devoid of high ground and ideally suited to airfield construction.

Initially eight airfields, and a headquarters constructed for an RAF Bomber Command Group to the west of the town of Huntingdon, were turned over to the heavy bombers. As the force expanded, airfields under construction to the east in the counties of Norfolk, Suffolk and Essex were embraced. The bomber airfields were good, and built to a standard pattern with three intersecting runways encircled by a perimeter track. Dispersal points for aircraft parking were accessible from various points along the perimeter track; these and the runways were of reinforced concrete with macadam surfacing. Base facilities and domestic sites were dispersed in the surrounding countryside, to minimise disruption in the event of a heavy enemy air attack. Each airfield had a high degree of self-sufficiency to prevent operations from being impeded should general power and other services fail. Camp facilities were of a utility nature but adequate. With economy in view, each airfield would support one heavy bombardment group which entailed adding extra dispersal points to older airfields so that fifty were available on each site.

Due to diversions to meet exigencies in the war against Japan, and shortages in crews and aircraft, the first heavy bombers did not start arriving until July 1942; but by the end of August 119 B-17s, the complement of the 97th, 301st and 92nd Groups, plus a score of reserves, had arrived in England. Most of the aircraft flew on the North Atlantic ferry route via Greenland and Iceland, although the 92nd Group made a direct 2,120 mile flight from Newfoundland to Scotland. Accompanying the first bombers came similar numbers of transports and fighters, the latter being the twin-engined P-38 Lightning, which had the best performance of all current AAF service fighters and a particularly useful range.

Both Spaatz and Eaker were anxious to get the heavy bombers into action at the earliest date and an intensive training programme ensued for the first group, the 97th, whose crews were untrained in many aspects of their duties, due to limited instructional facilities in the United States. One reason for hastening the combat debut was the desire to prove that the Fortresses really could perform effectively against strategic targets. U.S. forces operating in the Pacific, particularly the Navy, unconvinced that the defeat of Germany should be the first objective, objected to the diversion of resources to pursue the unproved theories of strategic bombing.

Early in August the 97th Bomb Group (BG) was ready for limited operations and on the 17th the first mission of the 8th AF was flown. Twelve B-17Es were despatched to bomb the large marshalling yard at Sotteville, near Rouen in north-east France, which handled military rail consignments for the area. As a gesture of faith in the ability of his bombers to do the job General Eaker flew as an observer in one of the Fortresses, while General Spaatz and many other high ranking British and American officers were on hand to watch the take-off and return of the small formation. The weather was fine and the B-17s dropped their 1,100 lb and 600 lb bombs from 23,000 feet, about half falling in the general target area and causing damage to rolling stock, buildings and track. The weight of the attack was insufficient to bring major devastation but for a first mission a reasonable degree of accuracy and success was shown. The bombers were provided with a strong escort of RAF fighters and returned without loss or battle damage.

Further missions by the 97th followed in quick succession, all without loss and usually with reasonably accurate bombing. These attacks involved only shallow penetration of hostile territory to permit RAF fighter cover. For while the 8th AF had high hopes that their bombers could eventually brave enemy fighters without escort, at this formative stage with such a small force – averaging fourteen – they were glad to receive the fighter protection that the RAF deemed so necessary. Targets were chiefly shipping installations, airfields and railyards; a far cry from the grandiose plan for striking German war industry, but a cautious programme had begun.

These early probing missions elated those AAF officers faithful to the cause of daylight precision bombardment. This was to some degree reflected

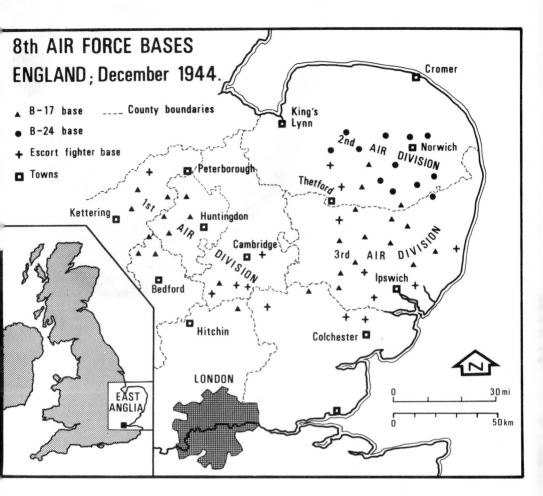

**8th AIR FORCE BASES
ENGLAND; December 1944.**

▲ B—17 base ---- County boundaries
● B—24 base
+ Escort fighter base
□ Towns

Cromer

King's Lynn

2nd AIR DIVISION Norwich

Peterborough

Thetford

Kettering 1st AIR DIVISION

Huntingdon

Cambridge

3rd AIR DIVISION

Bedford

Ipswich

Hitchin

Colchester

LONDON

EAST ANGLIA

N

0   30 mi
0   50 km

in a new AAF plan, AWPD-42, prepared at the end of August 1942 to meet a Presidential request for an up-to-date estimate of future air requirements. This spoke optimistically of a low attrition rate for U.S. bombers and a high one for intercepting fighters due to the heavy fire power of the former. AWPD-42 was in general an affirmation of the earlier AWPD-1 plan adjusted in the light of subsequent developments. The heavy toll U-boats were taking of transatlantic shipping made it imperative to quickly neutralise this threat. Primary objectives were now submarine yards, transportation, electric power, oil, aluminium and synthetic rubber, with the aircraft industry an intermediate objective.

Other plans were retarding the aims of AWPD-42. In July 1942 the Allies abandoned the proposed invasion of continental Europe in that year and the following, revising instead a plan to invade north-west Africa that autumn. The bulk of air units and equipment being supplied to the 8th AF would now be used for the American air contigent supporting the invasion (code-named TORCH). Subsequently this detached air element became the 12th AF, whose training and equipping fell largely to the 8th AF, so limiting their own operations from the U.K.

Nevertheless, the 8th AF still pressed its case for strategic bombing and continued operations. If operations had so far gone smoothly, there was still much to learn and numerous tactical and technical problems to solve. Of immediate concern was the poor standard of air crew training, manifest in the two groups (301st and 92nd) following the 97th BG to England. Both were equipped with the new B-17F Fortress, similar in appearance and performance to the B-17E model flown by the 97th, but vastly improved technically. The decision was made to use the 92nd BG as the basis of a combat crew replacement centre to provide the necessary operational training school through which all bomber crews would pass before entering combat. To this end the 92nd exchanged its B-17Fs for the 97th's B-17Es. To bolster the numbers on certain missions the 92nd BG was, in fact, called to undertake occasional operations during the fall of 1942.

On 5th September the 301st joined the 97th on operations, swelling the number of B-17s despatched to 37, while the following day, with a contribution from the 92nd BG, a force of fifty-four set out. The main force of forty one attacked the aircraft factory at Meaulte, France, while the secondary force from the 301st BG carried out a diversion raid on the enemy fighter airfield at St Omer. For the first time the Luftwaffe made a concerted effort to intercept, despite the Spitfire escort, and succeeded in shooting down two of the main force B-17s, inflicting the 8th AF's first heavy bomber loss.

Only two more missions were flown in September due to poor weather which prevented one attack being completed. In the meantime the two experienced groups, the 97th and 301st, all other equipped and trained groups in England and many on their way, together with a major proportion of personnel and support facilities were earmarked for the 12th AF. Six more heavy bombardment groups, scheduled to reach England during September, were to remain with the Eighth and it was hoped that they would be led into operations by the experienced groups before they were moved.

With weather considered suitable for precision attack on 9th October, a record force of 108 heavies were despatched including, for the first time, the 306th and 93rd BGs, the latter equipped with B-24 Liberators. The target was a major steel works at Lille. Due to the inexperience of many crews, deteriorating weather and other factors, only sixty-nine bombers dropped on the primary target and thirty-three did not bomb at all. Further, the bombing accuracy was not up to the usual standard although sufficient bombs landed on the target to cause substantial damage. An embarrassing aspect of the operation was the huge claims of enemy fighters destroyed and damaged made by the B-17 and B-24 gunners in the ensuing air battle. Initially these ran to fifty-six destroyed, twenty-six probably destroyed and twenty damaged, double the number of enemy fighters intelligence sources said could have been involved – as indeed was true.

In previous exchanges between enemy fighters and B-17s the high claims had been doubted; the Lille mission affirmed that claims assessment was badly inaccurate. The reason was not, as it may have seemed, bragging but the very nature of these high altitude battles. In a closely knit formation, it was possible for a score of gunners to fire at one fighter which, if hit, might be claimed in good faith by all. The sheer pace of combat with 600 mph closing speeds, restricted vision from some gun positions, use of oxygen masks, excitement and fear, all contributed to a distorted picture of events. The German tactic of rolling over and accelerating away in a dive – often accompanied by a burst of flame and smoke from the engine exhaust – was frequently taken to be a smitten fighter. Luftwaffe records show only two fighters lost in their attack which was a far cry from even the revised figures of VIII Bomber Command (VIII BC). German losses were, of course, unknown to the Allies at the time. If known, they would have had a demoralising effect on the American combatants who, even if suspicious of their claims, were nevertheless convinced that they were causing attrition among German fighter units.

While a strict procedure for making claims was introduced, and although adhered to in the months ahead, claims by the gunners remained inflated. This is not to underrate the defensive capabilities of the B-17 and B-24 which were remarkable. In these early battles the Luftwaffe soon appreciated the defensive fire as a formidable obstacle. The 0.50 calibre guns were effective at double the range of the 0.30 machine guns mainly used for Allied bomber defensive armament. A single round of 'fifty calibre' could inflict shattering airframe damage, whereas a 0.30 tended merely to 'hole'.

Since the Eighth Air Force was hopeful of establishing the validity of its mission, the destruction of large numbers of enemy fighters making banner headlines was good propaganda for the cause, as well as boosting aircrew morale. While in some respects these high figures were an embarrassment, it cannot be denied that they added weight to General Arnold's efforts to protect the programme for a strategic offensive.

Many problems that had come to light needed experimentation and exploration to solve. The untimely removal of the seasoned 97th and 301st Groups to North Africa in November meant that the task would fall to the new groups, the 306th, 91st, 305th and 303rd with B-17Fs, and the 93rd and 44th with B-24Ds – the last being at part strength, having had one of its squadrons transferred to Alaska before the group arrived in Britain.

Spaatz had been elevated to command all U.S. African air commands, leaving Eaker to mind the 8th AF. Both Spaatz and Eaker were optimistic, for on the strength of early bombing results it was estimated that 25 per cent of bombs could be placed within 250 yards of the aiming point. Eaker was enthusiastic enough to suggest that given twenty groups the 8th AF and RAF Bomber Command could completely disrupt German war industry and commerce. This optimism was unwarranted in the light of subsequent events; Eaker was not to have known that during the following six months the effects of sustaining the North African venture would seriously impede his campaign. Indeed, the inroads into 8th AF personnel and supplies had already been felt. Nowhere was the position more serious than in replacement crews and aircraft, the trickle reaching the U.K. being inadequate to meet operational losses. The winter of 1942–43 was very much the season of the 'hangar queen', whereby it was necessary to rob disabled aircraft of parts to keep others flying. Replacements for the B-24 units were practically non-existent, forcing some squadrons to all but cease operations.

The demands of the North African campaign early in 1943 took two more of the B-17 groups originally destined for the U.K. and the B-24 equipped 93rd Group (less one squadron engaged in a bad weather nuisance raids experiment) was detached to the 12th AF and 9th AF (USAAF in Middle East) until March 1943. The remaining B-24 group, the 44th, which had commenced operating in November 1942, was too small a force to be effectively employed on its own, or jointly with B-17s due to differing performances.

While Eaker had been pleased to receive groups equipped with both types of bomber, the problems of operating them in the same bomber stream were difficult. Although the B-24's service ceiling was 28,000 feet, high wing loading of operationally loaded aircraft made it difficult to keep in formation above 21,000 feet, some 4,000 feet below the optimum B-17 level. Additionally, the B-24D's cruising speed under these conditions, 10 mph faster than the Fortress's, caused problems in mission timing. One method of employing them with B-17s to attack the same target was for them to bring up the rear. Unhappily their lower, exposed position, led the enemy to select their formations for interception on several occasions; a commander of one of the early B-17 groups said quite seriously, 'With B-24s around, who needs escort!' There was more than an element of truth in this jibe. For this reason the Liberators were often used for heavily escorted diversion attacks, leaving the four B-17 groups to carry the torch for strategic bombardment during this phase of the war.

The target directives for the 8th AF were not far out of line with AWPD-42, giving priority to attacks on submarine facilities extending along the western coast of France, from where the enemy might harass shipping supporting TORCH. Second priority was given to aircraft facilities, factories, repair depots and airfields supporting the Luftwaffe. Transportation targets took third place. Thus the submarine support bases of Lorient, La Pallice and St Nazaire received particular attention for three months, but weather and deficiencies in strength limited this part of the campaign to sixteen effective missions. These Atlantic ports became the breaking-in ground for the new groups, although heavy anti-aircraft defences made them increasingly dangerous targets. Approach from the sea did mitigate losses and damage which, on occasions, were high due to heavy concentrations of anti-aircraft guns which elsewhere had not proved a formidable obstacle.

One major mission not against submarine installations, was flown to the Luftwaffe aircraft depot at Romilly-sur-Seine near Paris on 20th December. The long-range missions to the Atlantic coast ports had shown that the B-17s could fight off enemy interceptors, but the Romilly mission was the first where the bombers penetrated hostile airspace for a substantial distance without benefit of fighter escort. As soon as Spitfires had reached the limit of their escort and left the bombers, enemy fighters began persistent attacks that continued to the target and on return until RAF fighters relieved the situation. From the force of 101 despatched, six B-17s were lost and another two written off in crash landings in the U.K. as a result of damage sustained. As most of the Luftwaffe interceptors in France were airborne that day the mission gave weight to the belief that the bombers could fight their way through to a target without fighter escort. While this had been accepted in war plans, fighter escort also figured in the original promotion of a strategic bomber offensive from England.

There had been hope that two P-38F Lightning groups, that had arrived in the U.K. with the early B-17s, could be used for escort as they had a radius of action of 210 miles, to the RAF Spitfires' 150 miles. The original P-38s had been sent to North Africa but another group, arriving in December, was

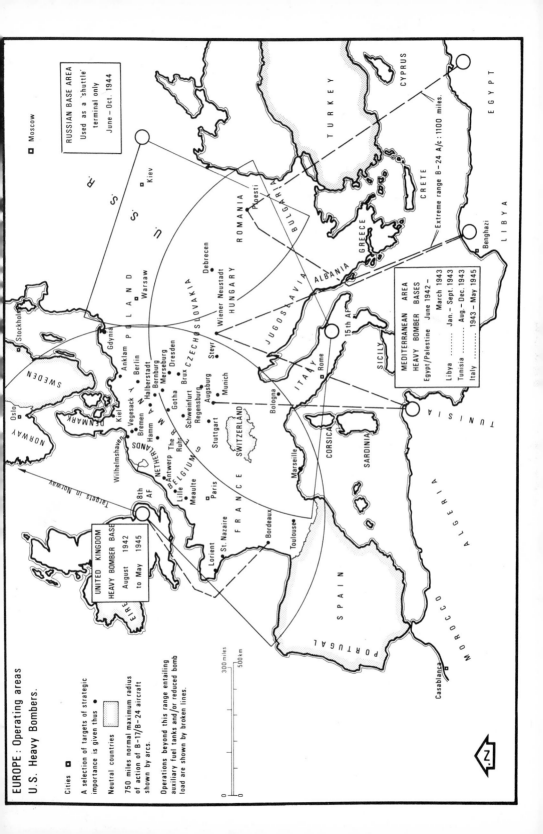

EUROPE : Operating areas
U.S. Heavy Bombers.

Cities ■

A selection of targets of strategic
importance is given thus ●

Neutral countries [ ]

750 miles normal maximum radius
of action of B-17/B-24 aircraft
shown by arcs.

Operations beyond this range entailing
auxiliary fuel tanks and/or reduced bomb
load are shown by broken lines.

0 ___ 300 miles
0 ___ 500 km

■ Moscow

RUSSIAN BASE AREA
Used as a 'shuttle'
terminal only
June – Oct. 1944

UNITED KINGDOM
HEAVY BOMBER BASE
August 1942
to May 1945

MEDITERRANEAN
AREA
HEAVY BOMBER
BASES
Egypt/Palestine June 1942 –
                              March 1943
Libya .... Jan. – Sept. 1943
Tunisia .... Aug. – Dec. 1943
Italy .... 1943 – May 1945

Extreme range B-24 A/c : 1100 miles.

8th AF

15th AF

Targets in Norway

Labels on map

NORWAY
SWEDEN
Stockholm
Oslo
DENMARK
EIRE
NETHERLANDS
BELGIUM
FRANCE
SWITZERLAND
SPAIN
PORTUGAL
ITALY
CORSICA
SARDINIA
SICILY
TUNISIA
ALGERIA
MOROCCO
LIBYA
EGYPT
CYPRUS
CRETE
GREECE
ALBANIA
JUGOSLAVIA
BULGARIA
ROMANIA
HUNGARY
CZECHOSLOVAKIA
POLAND
U.S.S.R.

Kiel
Vegesack
Bremen
Wilhelmshaven
Anklam
Gdynia
Berlin
Halberstadt
Bernburg
Merseburg
Dresden
Hamm
Ruhr
The Ruhr
Antwerp
Lille
Meaulte
Paris
St. Nazaire
Lorient
Bordeaux
Toulouse
Marseille
Gotha
Schweinfurt
Regensburg
Stuttgart
Augsburg
Munich
Brux
Steyr
Wiener Neustadt
Debrecen
Warsaw
Kiev
Ploesti
Rome
Bologna
Benghazi
Casablanca

assigned to the Eighth. Unfortunately losses in North Africa quickly demanded all P-38s and pilots in the U.K. as replacements. In lieu of the P-38s the new P-47 Thunderbolt fighter was sent to Europe; early in 1943 three groups were established to operate this untried fighter, although teething troubles and radio modifications delayed its true operational debut until April. Even then, the type offered a radius of action of 175 miles which, an advance on the Spitfire, was much less than that of the P-38. The P-47's range could be improved by auxiliary disposable fuel tanks, a possibility investigated by the 8th AF Technical Section during the spring of 1943

For the immediate future the B-17s and B-24s had to rely on their own defensive armament to ward off enemy fighters on deep penetrations From the outset there had been inadequate armament, notably in the nose of the bombers where only a single rifle-calibre machine gun was provided. As the Japanese had quickly discovered in the early days of air combat in the south-west Pacific, frontal assaults on the U.S. heavies could be less hazardous and more successful than conventional attacks from the rear although demanding greater skill and nerve due to the high rate of closure. Such attacks were first experienced by 8th AF on a mission to St. Nazaire in November 1942 and thereafter were frequently encountered, although this form of attack was initially practised by the Jagdgeschwader defending the Paris area. The fitting of one or two 0.50 calibre weapons in the nose position of most B-17s and B-24s was an intermediate step to counter this threat, but the installation was cumbersome and limited in field of fire. There was need for a power-operated nose turret. In the autumn of 1942 the 8th AF had modified a B-17E to take B-24 tail turrets in nose and tail, as an experiment in improving armament. The idea of an extra heavily armed bomber to act as escort gun platform on the flanks of formation was also explored, resulting in a dozen prepared in the U.S. for trials with the 8th AF.

Collective defence depended greatly on the pattern of the formation and in early operations each group had its own ideas on the most effective form. A concerted effort was made in January 1943 to assess the most desirable formation and to adopt a standard. By experimenting with aircraft stacked up and down, and from left to right in echelon, forming a wedge-shaped formation to give the widest field of fire to the maximum number of guns, the basic defensive formation was established. This was a group or box of eighteen or twenty-one aircraft. Theoretically, the larger the formation the better its defensive potential, but in practice large formations were unwieldy in manoeuvring. Two or three group boxes would form a large defensive assembly known as a combat wing.

Gunnery was poor – despite the large claims in combat – and local training was performed whenever possible. Aerial gunnery was a skill not easily acquired; deflection shooting required aiming in advance of, not at, an attacking fighter. Practice improved gunnery standards, but the best air gunners were natural marksmen anyway. During an air battle it was not uncommon for bombers in a formation to suffer damage from 'friendly' fire, particularly by waist gunners riddling the tailplane of their own aircraft. If the standard of gunnery fell far short of the ideal, the massed firepower of twenty to thirty guns presented a formidable barrage for an attacking fighter to penetrate.

In developing defensive formations consideration had to be paid to

One B-17 squadron battle formation. Basic element of all formations was a 3-plane-vee flight.

Brigadier General Haywood Hansell and Colonel Curtis LeMay, VIII Bomber Command wing and group commanders respectively, at the time of this photo, May 1943. Both later featured prominently in the direction of the strategic bombing of Japan.

target approach for bombing. During the early operations each B-17 equipped with a Norden sight manned by a bombardier, broke formation for the bombing run. Bombers were then very vulnerable, a fact not lost on the enemy. A new tactic was therefore tried. During the bomb run only the lead and deputy lead aircraft of a group or squadron, dependent on the size of the formation, would have a bombardier and bomb sight; all the other aircraft in the formation dropped visually on their leader's release. In this way, not only could defensive formations be maintained, but the technique provided a better bomb pattern from each unit and allowed the most experienced bombardiers to be used in the lead aircraft. Following on from this came lead crews, specially groomed teams who stood a better chance of effecting a good strike for the unit.

Accuracy, the most important factor, could be achieved from altitudes around 25,000 feet in good visibility. Prior to America's entry into the war the Norden bombsight had been developed in conjunction with a mechanism that allowed the bombardier directional control of the bomber on the bombing run. Known as AFCE (Automatic Flight Control Equipment) it coupled the bombsight to the automatic pilot and gave the bombardier more assured control of the aircraft during vital alignment with the target. But AFCE had teething troubles and was not in general operational use until the spring of 1943. An alternative method was through directions indicated visually in the cockpit on the PDI (Pilots' Directional Indicator) for the pilot to make flight adjustments required by the bombardier. The bombing run was commenced from a turn at a preselected landmark called the IP (Initial Point) and no more than a three minute run was desirable, as the straight approach gave flak defences an opportunity to set their guns accordingly.

Over the weather there was no control. Aware from meteorological advisers that an average of five 'fine' days was likely in any one month during the European winter, the 8th AF commanders found their initial experience a particularly cloudy period. Weather over the British Isles is generally moderate, but highly variable with sudden changes in temperature. While the average winter month may produce five fine days, the average often bears little resemblance to any actual period. In early 1943 the weather was inhospitable with a good deal of fog; even when the sun shone over France or Germany the bombers might be 'socked in' at their bases. The British had developed weather reporting to a fine art but this could not always foretell that a fine early morning would become overcast by midday. Often the bombers would reach their objective only to find it veiled by cloud, leaving the alternative of finding secondary targets or those of opportunity, or returning with their bombs. Weather was undoubtedly the most frustrating factor for the commanders and men and the greatest obstacle to accurate bombing.

A related aspect was the effect of the high humidity in north-west Europe at this time of year. Moisture penetrating items of clothing and oxygen masks would freeze at high altitude with uncomfortable results. Guns would fail to function and bomb release mechanisms often iced up. Moisture, collected at lower altitudes and freezing at higher realms, also affected engine components although the B-17s and B-24s were not troubled as seriously in this respect as fighter types. All these problems were overcome but some took many months to solve.

Tactical and technical problems beset the 8th AF bombers on most missions during the winter of 1942–43; 25,000 feet over north-west Europe was a rough proving ground. Anxious to see the bombers strike into Germany – for their own and national prestige – 8th AF extended their ventures to submarine installations along the north German coast. This objective at this stage stemmed from the Casablanca conference of early January 1943, where General Eaker had been asked, perhaps critically, why his bombers had so far refrained from venturing over the enemy homeland.

An 8th AF combat wing formation en route to Germany. High and low groups are compact but lead group is spread out with one bomber lagging far behind.

The meeting between the British and American leaders at Casablanca was for a reappraisal of strategy. An issue raised by some members of the British contingent was the desirability of having 8th AF bombers join RAF Bomber Command in night raids on Germany. To counter this move General Arnold, who had attended with Roosevelt from the U.S., sent for Eaker, who could speak from experience on the value of the daylight attacks. The 8th AF commander pointed out that currently night bombers sustained a higher loss rate than the day bombers whose bombing accuracy he estimated as five times better. Eaker, a skilled diplomat, expanded his case, impressing Prime Minister Churchill with his suggestion of 'round the clock bombing' in which the 8th AF and RAF Bomber Command could conduct a complementary campaign of destruction to the enemy, giving him no respite. Favourably impressed with the case for pounding Germany from the air until such time as a cross-Channel invasion could be mounted, the Casablanca Conference provided the first directive with positive endorsement from Allied leaders for a combined bomber offensive from the United

Kingdom. The primary objectives listed were, in order of priority: the submarine construction yards, aircraft industry, transportation, oil plants and other targets in enemy war industry. A more detailed directive on a Combined Bomber Offensive would be issued at a later date after investigation by experts. To co-ordinate policy, the overall control of the offensive would be vested in Air Chief Marshal Sir Charles Portal.

The RAF had been operating over Germany since 1940 although, like the 8th AF, it had been diverted from strategic objectives and was currently concentrating about half its total effort against maritime targets, reflecting the grave situation on the high seas where the destruction of shipping by U-boats had been running at an alarming rate. Now given first priority, these targets were receiving nearly a third of the total RAF bombing effort and over two-thirds of that of the 8th AF by the beginning of 1943. Six days after the Casablanca directive was issued, came the first American mission to Germany when, on 27th January, ninety-one B-17s and B-24s set out to bomb the U-boat yards at Wilhelmshaven. While only fifty-three attacked, the bombing appeared accurate but a particularly pleasing aspect was the comparatively light loss of three bombers, and two of these were B-24s from a lone unit that wandered badly off course. This initial reaction to the violation of German air space was to be an exception.

The rate of operations was often slow through missions being abandoned in their early stages due to deteriorating weather. The limitations of winter weather apart, the rate of operations was conditioned by the rate of replacements, men and aircraft. Only three major missions were completed during February although a dozen were scheduled, and brought losses which averaged over 13 per cent of the bombers attacking. One of the abandoned missions was to have been the deepest penetration so far into the Reich, with an attack on marshalling yards at Hamm in the heavily defended area. Another attempt made on 4th March was largely frustrated by weather; haze and cloud caused three of the four B-17 groups to abandon the primary objective. The fourth group, the 91st BG, apparently unaware it was alone, later emerged into clear weather and continued to the target to make an accurate drop. This small formation of fourteen suffered for its audacity, being under almost constant fighter attack on the return flight, losing four. The heroics of this mission proved a valuable lift to morale for the group concerned but its total loss of five bombers and considerable damage to others showed again the vulnerability of small formations.

Losses during March and April missions were generally under 5 per cent, which was considered an acceptable rate. There was one notable exception, the 17th April raid on the Focke-Wulf aircraft factory at Bremen when sixteen B-17s failed to return from the force of 106 bombing, the largest concentration so far over any one target. Early assessment of the bombers' objective enabled the German fighter control to assemble some sixty fighters for a concentrated assault during the bomb run, primarily against the low group of the leading combat wing which incurred most of the losses. A post-mission critique revealed that the leading formations, too strung out, did not have the compactness affording the best defence. Even so, while the VIII BC might commendably seek its own weaknesses and endeavour to eliminate them, through regular post-mission critiques, the success of the German defences could be attributed to recent improvements on their part.

Anti-aircraft fire – *Flak* – was regularly encountered and at some targets, such as St Nazaire, was quite formidable. Nevertheless flak was the known cause of only 14 per cent of losses although some 60 per cent of battle damage sustained by returning bombers could be attributed to this weapon. The greater proportion of losses during the winter of 1942–43, however, were due to fighter attack.

Fighter defence had passed through notable phases. In the early exploratory raids, under heavy RAF Spitfire escort, the Luftwaffe discreetly awaited an opportunity. They attacked only when, through bad timing or other contingencies, the Spitfires were not at hand. Tactics included feints to draw the escort into battle while the main force of German fighters intercepted the bombers or, in raids where the bombers ventured beyond the range of their escorts, waiting until the escort withdrew. The German fighter force in the west, at this time limited to some 120 fighters in France and the Low Countries, was prudently used and avoided engagements with numerically superior forces of Allied fighters. After discovering the hazards of flanking attacks through the bombers' concentrated defensive fire, the more experienced Luftwaffe units met the bombers head-on, finding return fire weakest in that quarter. Attacks made at first by fighters in pairs, a

Two 2,000 lb GP M34 bombs being pushed under the bay of a veteran 303rd BG B-17F. These were the largest weapons a Fortress could carry internally.

standard Luftwaffe method, were countered by the bombers' evasive action; but this in turn was countered by assailing the bombers with waves of four, six or eight aircraft at a time, so that in avoiding alignment with one fighter, the bomber might move into the sights of another. This tactic became a regular attack feature with many units.

The Luftwaffe quickly recognized that the first objective was to disperse a bomber box, thus making the destruction of individual aircraft a much easier task. Among techniques tried early in 1943 were dropping time-fused bombs into formations, trailing explosive devices on cables and persistent experiments with air-launched 210 mm infantry rockets. Twin-engined fighters with heavier armament offered promise, particularly armed with weapons out-ranging the bombers' 0.50 calibre guns. German studies showed that on average twenty 20 mm cannon shell strikes were necessary to bring down a B-17, such was the sturdy construction. As considerable damage could be sustained without its destruction, heavier calibre guns appeared necessary. An immediate requirement was more fighters; despite pressures on the Russian front a movement of fighters to the west began in the early spring of 1943.

In March 1943 the effective combat strength of VIII BC improved as the North African campaign ceased to make inroads into logistics, and more replacements were forthcoming from the United States. While exigencies in Africa had deprived the 8th AF of two B-17 groups in February, and those of the Pacific two B-24 groups in March and April, VIII BC did have its combat strength doubled when four new B-17 groups arrived during April. That same month the 92nd BG, which had been used as the basis of the bomber combat crew replacement unit at Bovingdon, reformed as a combat unit with one squadron equipped with YB-40 'gun ships'. The Liberator groups were brought up to full strength, the 93rd having returned from its detachment in North Africa (originally to be only a few weeks, but lasting two and a half months) to give Eaker a total of 500 bombers – half operational – by early May and a force more fitted for the difficult task ahead.

A bombing mission to the Ford vehicle works at Antwerp on 4th May without loss was a milestone in that U.S. P-47 fighters performed their first escort. The raid also marked the last occasion when the main combat requirement would be provided by the four B-17 groups that for the previous six months had constituted Bomber Command's principal strike element. These groups had pioneered much of the practical doctrine for conducting high level bombardment operations, proving sound enough to remain little changed to the conclusion of hostilities.

The criterion of success was bombing results which, with experience and enhanced technique, had shown gradual improvement in the number of hits within a thousand feet of the planned aiming point. The average had grown encouragingly from under 15 per cent to more than 20 per cent. On the occasion the 305th BG attacked Vegesack submarine yards, on 18th March 1943, it reached as high as 76 per cent. Photographic reconnaissance sorties (at that time undertaken by the RAF) had provided indisputable evidence of the accuracy of attacks but there was too great a tendency to equate accuracy with destruction. Interpretation of damage shown in aerial photographs, although developed to a fine art, was invariably too optimistic,

for facilities that were adjudged to have been put out of action for several months were often back to full capacity within a few weeks.

Some 25,000 feet over Germany, an Me 109 dives away after delivering an attack on a straggling B-17 of 94th BG.

Submarine facilities had been the principal targets during the experimental period and here more than anywhere an inflated picture of the destruction achieved existed. From the outset there had been little hope of smashing the thick concrete shelters protecting operational U-boat bases, but the attacks were thought to have so mutilated dockside support facilities that the enemy would have great difficulty in maintaining and refitting his vessels. While some disorganisation resulted from the raids, there is no evidence of any appreciable decline in U-boat operations attributable to them. Likewise the submarine building programme did not suffer adversely despite attacks such as the spectacular bombing of the construction yard at Vegesack in March, where half the hulls visible were thought to be severely damaged. In fact, none were beyond economical repair and within six weeks production capacity was near normal. Results against aircraft and vehicle plants had been more telling in the destruction wrought, but again the Allies failed to recognise the recuperative ability of their enemy. A major factor conditioning the bombing results of the B-17 and B-24s in Europe was the limited bomb size; a deficiency not fully appreciated until later in the war. A large percentage of the loads were composed of 500 and 1,000 lb high explosive bombs which lacked the destructive capacity necessary to mangle machine tools and heavy construction equipment except by a direct hit.

This is not to underrate the bombing of the experimental period for had been carried out with an average effective strength of ninety bombers far short of the necessary 300 called for in AAF plans for a strike against single major target. A greater weight of bombs would obviously have produced more telling results. Suffice that in May 1943 the position appeared rosier than it actually was. To the 8th AF commanders the opening month of the campaign, fraught with difficulties and conducted in inadequate strength, had proved that the day bomber could venture unescorted into the most formidable air environment of any war front. While the 'friendly opposition' may not have been convinced, they had little ground for contesting the allocation of so large a part of the U.S. war economy to supply the larger bomber fleets still required.

At this time the 8th AF commanders were confident that with their new-found strength they could really show what the strategic bomber could achieve. There was no less enthusiasm with General Arnold and his advisors in Washington, but perhaps more critical concern. The 8th AF was the major air commitment of the AAF and placed where it could establish once and for all that long cherished independent role for air power.

May-October 1943: The Great Fortress Battles

The period between early May and the end of October 1943 was the most crucial for proving the American day bomber's ability to survive on its assigned mission without fighter support. A succession of engagements between the bombers and enemy fighters ensued, bringing some of the most intense air battles of history.

By 12th May the groups that had recently joined VIII BC were ready for operations, giving Eaker over 200 bombers to commit to battle. Two groups were initiated the following day in a diversionary raid on a Channel coast airfield while the main force, including the rejuvenated 92nd BG attacked the aircraft plant at Meaulte in France. But it was 14th May that brought the pattern of future operations with the first major display of this greatly enhanced striking power – 224 heavy and eleven medium bombers were sent to four targets.

Deception from the outset had featured in VIII BC planning. Sometimes the bomber force would make feints towards one target, and attack another perhaps divide and hit two targets or, more commonly, one small force heavily escorted, would try to draw the enemy fighters away from the main effort. Such ruses were sometimes resoundingly successful, sometimes disastrous failures, but overall advantageous. They were a valuable ploy because the endurance of German interceptors was about $1\frac{1}{2}$ hours on internal fuel supply; once committed to one sector they might well have to land to refuel before journeying elsewhere. The bombers could penetrate anywhere along a thousand-mile coastline, forcing wide dispersion of Luftwaffe fighter units When German fighter controllers recognised the main thrusts and objectives sufficiently early, fighters could be directed from other sectors to reinforce local units. The preliminaries of each day's mission became a battle of wits that could significantly affect the numbers of bombers that would fall in combat.

With his enlarged force Eaker could, as on 14th May, attack different targets to increase the chances of confusing the enemy. Additionally RAF

light bombers and fighters co-operated with operations timed to draw the opposition from the American heavies. The new groups went to Antwerp, and Courtrai airfield, to pin down fighters in northern France and the Low Countries, while the main force went to Kiel submarine yards. The mediums, Martin B-26 Marauders, attacked a power station in Holland, in extreme contrast to the heavies, by going in at 'hedge-hopping' heights. While the day's bombing was variable, losses would have been comparatively light but for the fate of the unfortunate 44th B-24 group bringing up the rear of the Kiel force and losing six aircraft to concentrated enemy attacks. Flying several hundred feet below the Fortresses and lacking their firepower support, the losses of this unit again showed the dangers attendant on operating a small formation without some form of cover.

On the 17th May, while the B-17s went to Lorient, the two B-24 groups despatched 39 aircraft and fared well. Thereafter they were assigned to special training and detached to North Africa to undertake an audacious mission to Ploesti (see page 64). The first new B-24 group for eight months, arrived in the U.K. in June and soon flew on to join the other two groups in North Africa.

To facilitate control VIII BC groups were organised under intermediate headquarters called wings. The B-24 units had been concentrated under the 2nd Bomb Wing since late in 1942, and some of the new B-17 groups arriving in April 1943 under the 4th Bomb Wing, which was generally briefed for a different target to B-17s of the old 1st Bomb Wing. The B-26 mediums were assigned to the 3rd Bomb Wing. The 8th AF would have preferred additional heavy to medium bombers, particularly as the B-26 units were trained along the lines so successfully employed in the south-west Pacific

Air-to-air rocket projectiles exploding beyond a 381st BG B-17 formation. The German fighter pilots misjudged range on this occasion.

in recent months. This involved very low-level operation, the aircraft having extra fixed forward-firing armament for strafing as they attacked. Using these bombers in this fashion was questionable due to the extremely proficient and dense anti-aircraft defences in the Low Countries and France, where the RAF had long discovered such tactics were only viable if extremely fast light bombers were used, exploiting the element of surprise. The B-26s' debut on 14th May not only resulted in heavy battle damage, causing one returning bomber to crash near its base, but the mission failed completely because no bombs hit the target at Ijmuiden. A second attempt made on 17th May was disastrous; of the eleven aircraft reaching Holland none returned. Apparently a gross navigational error bringing them over the heavy flak defences of the Maas estuary precipitated the disaster. After this the B-26s were moved to VIII Air Support Command with the intention of employing them later in medium level bombardment in a largely tactical role.

The new B-17 groups proved to have a much higher standard of training. Even so, their performance was erratic during early operations. There was no substitute for experience; although more proficient in their role, the crews did not have the advantage of the less violent introduction that attended the baptism of the earlier groups. Not only was the Luftwaffe offering more determined resistance, its seasoned units knew how best to exploit the weakness of poorly assembled bomber formations not uncommon in some of the new groups. Air discipline was being taught the hard way. One of the worst debacles suffered by the 4th Bomb Wing groups was on the 13th June mission to Kiel where of twenty-six B-17s lost that day, twenty-two were from these groups. The mission was one of the opening blows in the Combined Bomber Offensive (CBO).

Authorised at the Casablanca conference early in January, and although target priorities listed then had formed a basis for operational planning ever since, the official directive was not forthcoming until 10th June. A careful analysis of the German war economy by a strategic study group, in conjunction with other interested agencies, took many weeks. The CBO plan varied slightly the priorities as follows. Intermediate objective: German fighter strength. Primary objectives: submarine yards and bases, the remainder of the German aircraft industry, ball bearings and oil. Secondary objectives: synthetic rubber and tyres, military motor transport vehicles.

Ball bearings were considered a vulnerable item, as more than 50 per cent of production stemmed from factories at Schweinfurt. The Germans were believed to have no great reserve stocks so that the destruction of the few main plants might quickly affect aircraft and fighting vehicle production. Synthetic rubber was the basis of most German tyres, natural rubber supplies being assessed as small. Here again a specialised product with ten known principal sources could have serious consequences on aircraft and vehicle production if subjected to telling bombardment. Submarine facilities had first priority but such was the success in improved anti-submarine techniques at sea during the spring of 1943, that from June VIII BC would make little effort in that direction. Also, intelligence gained from the French underground movement and other sources indicated that attacks on these targets were largely ineffectual.

For the American contingent, the CBO plan also recommended the size of the forces required to carry out the task, to be completed before the cross-Channel invasion tentatively set for a suitable date from 1st May 1944. A figure of 2,702 heavy bombers in fifty-one groups was to be deployed in the U.K. by 31st March 1944. In fact, in the summer of 1943, the AAF fixed the ultimate number of heavy bomber groups scheduled for the 8th AF at fifty-six with over three thousand B-17s and B-24s.

At least the build-up of such a force was being given some credence at the time the CBO plan was issued. In April 1943 the B-17 force on hand had jumped from under 200 to 350 with the arrival of the new groups. Additional units following in June and July raised the total to nearly 600, but thereafter there was a lull in expansion until November. With the B-24 groups absent from the U.K., the American contribution to the CBO was carried out by the Fortresses through the summer and early autumn, the sixteen groups being divided up into nine in the 1st Bomb Wing and seven in the 4th. In view of the projected size of VIII BC – three-quarters of all USAAF heavy bomb groups – and to avoid an unwieldy organisation, it was planned to divide the bomber command into four bombardment divisions. In effect this was a change of title for the Bombardment Wings, which already had their assigned groups organised into combat wings, ie battle formations, for tactical purposes. The official change was made in September.

The most successful of the nine operations in June, and 8th AF's first large-scale venture into the Ruhr, was to a synthetic rubber factory on the 22nd. Of the 235 B-17s despatched, 183 bombed and probably only a fifth of these effectively, but the damage was considerable, putting the plant out of action for a month. The inflammable nature of the product made it particularly vulnerable to bombing yet, presumably because this was a secondary priority target in the CBO, there were no follow-up attacks during 1943, the plant getting back to full production by the end of the year. June 1943 being unusually cloudy, deep penetrations into Germany were limited. Not until late July did a short period of fine weather permit what became known among the U.S. combatants as 'Blitz Week'. Following a strike at submarine facilities and other targets in Norway on 24th July, the B-17s struck deep into Germany, often 300 strong, on the 25th, 26th, 28th, 29th and 30th. The targets included submarine yards and docks, munitions and aircraft factories. On the 28th the 4th Bomb Wing made the deepest penetration of the Reich yet, some 200 miles inland to attack the FW190 assembly plant at Oschersleben, 90 miles south of Berlin. Unfortunately on this and other days weather deteriorated in the target areas, keeping some formations from finding their primary objectives. The B-17Fs of the 4th Bomb Wing had extra fuel cells in the outer wing sections, extending their radius of action by 300 miles. The older groups of 1st Bomb Wing were unable to reach such distant targets until their original aircraft had been replaced.

The missions of Blitz Week were marked by furious air battles bringing heavy losses to the bombers, but at the same time air gunners genuinely believed they were decimating the Luftwaffe. While their claims were highly inaccurate they were, nonetheless, causing losses amounting to a painful attrition even in the strengthened Luftwaffe fighter force in the west now numbering 600 Me109 and FW190 interceptors. Approximately forty German fighters were lost as a result of combat with B-17s during July against the gunners' claims of 545. The American loss was 128 B-17s, a

5.5 per cent loss ratio of aircraft entering hostile airspace, a rate which more than absorbed replacements. June, in fact, had been higher at over 6 per cent.

The YB-40 gun platform development of the B-17, flown in the exposed positions of bomber boxes during the past two months, proved a disappointment and was withdrawn. A promising development during Blitz Week, was the first successful use of expendable fuel tanks by the American fighter escort. P-47 Thunderbolts, hitherto limited in range to shallow penetrations of France and the Low Countries, were able to fly over the borders of Germany with the aid of these tanks and in the process caught one Luftwaffe fighter unit unawares. Fighter escort was undoubtedly the best means of reducing bomber losses and every effort was made to increase availability. Despite their own wounds in July battles, the 8th AF still believed the losses suffered by the Luftwaffe were crippling, and that one day soon there would be signs of such demise.

Two weeks were to pass before recuperation and the weather allowed another mission, this time to industrial targets in the Ruhr where twenty-five losses were incurred, the highest since June. A notable operation launched on August 17th resulted in excellent bombing, but a dramatic increase in losses. Originating as a combined operation with the B-24 groups in North Africa, against centres of fighter production, the ambitious plan was amended and flown solely by the 8th AF. Two parallel forces of B-17s, one from each division, were to simultaneously attack the ball bearing factories at Schweinfurt and the Messerschmitt fighter assembly plant at Regensburg. Both targets entailed longer flights over the enemy homeland than any previous, over 550 miles from England. The two task forces totalled 376 B-17s, a new high for bombers despatched. Diversion raids and maximum escort were arranged, but once the P-47s had turned back the Luftwaffe struck hard and continued to harass. The Regensburg force did not return to England, but turned south across the Mediterranean to land in North Africa, losing thirty-six bombers some of which having run out of fuel were forced down into the sea. The Schweinfurt force returned to England with twenty-four of its number lost. The combined total of sixty bombers lost was 19 per cent of the effective sorties! The mission was judged successful because of the excellent bombing, particularly at Regensburg. Damage to both plants was extensive and caused serious disruption for many weeks. The 4th Bomb Wing returned to England a week later, bombing a target in France on the way. The so-called 'shuttle' mission to Africa was not repeated, primarily because of the poor support facilities at the African airfields.

The majority of September's missions were directed at targets in occupied countries, chiefly airfields to support a plan to deceive the enemy into believing an invasion of the Pas de Calais was imminent and reveal his plans for invasion reaction. A major exception was an attempt to hit targets in the Stuttgart area on the 6th. A force of over 300 met with bad weather causing individual boxes to become detached from the bomber stream and then be viciously attacked by fighters. Additional losses were caused by bombers running out of fuel. The dubious bombing results at various targets of opportunity did not justify the loss of forty-five B-17s.

Missions of early October marked the peak of the 1943 air battles. Although the latest jettisonable fuel tanks allowed the expanded force of P-47s to fly over 300 miles from their bases to protect the heavies, the uftwaffe concentrated its forces beyond the reach of friendly fighters and attacked the bombers with even greater ferocity. The missions of 8th, 9th and 10th brought losses of thirty, twenty-eight and thirty bombers respectively. On each occasion the enemy concentrated on one or two groups at a time and in some cases almost completely eliminating them. On the first of three operations 309 bombers had been despatched but losses and damage incurred were such that when on the 14th another mission was launched, only 291 B-17s could be sent.

The objective was again the Schweinfurt bearing complex which some 400 enemy fighters rose to defend. An epic battle developed resulting in the loss of sixty B-17s, nearly 20 per cent of those despatched and almost 30 per cent of those attacking, pushing the average for October's operations to 9.2 per cent of credit sorties, a point near to which it had been considered too costly to operate. On the other hand the bombing results were excellent with a high concentration of hits on the manufacturing shops causing extensive damage which was judged to have completely halted production. It was a proud boast of the U.S. bomber men that never once had they been turned back from their objectives during the campaign. This was true, but the German fighters had now made the raids costly enough to be almost prohibitive. Even the most hardened advocate of the go-it-alone bomber doctrine had to concede that the B-17s, however well armed and armoured, were no match for the fighter opposition being encountered. That the heavy bombers were never again directed to a distant target without planned fighter support was due to the availability of such long range escort in the closing months of 1943. The battle for Schweinfurt did not stop the VIII BC's offensive; once ranks had been closed the winter weather was responsible for the lull that followed.

Smoke rising from the smitten Messerschmitt factory at Regensburg, as viewed through the waist window of a 385th BG B-17 flying at 24,000 feet.

Pathfinder B-17G of 96th BG on a target run with bomb bay doors open and H2S radome fully extended.

Operations during the early winter of 1943–44 were notable for the use of various pathfinder and radar devices to enable bombing to be carried out through an undercast. Of particular interest was the British H2S airborne radar which produced an image of prominent ground features on a cathode-ray tube in the aircraft. This blind bombing and navigational aid was invaluable in extending VIII BC operations to days of doubtful weather, allowing a mission to be launched when visual means could not be used. The radar devices were at first operated by a specially formed pathfinder group, the 482nd, which supplied the specially equipped bombers and crews to lead orthodox formations. Eventually, as more bombers with H2X (the U.S.-made version of H2S) became available, pathfinder units were established in each division, then each combat wing and finally in each group. Pathfinder lead bombing in its infancy was generally unreliable and could only be used against clearly definable areas – such as ports which produced significant contrast on the H2X screen between land and water.

Strategic Bombing Operations from Africa

Overall, 8th AF B-24 Liberator groups had not played a significant part in the operations from the U.K. prior to October 1943. Not only was their effective strength rarely more than forty aircraft, but on three occasions substantial numbers were detached to the Mediterranean theatre. The fire brigade of the heavy bomber team, they were rushed to deal with contingencies in campaigns that took the Allies to victory in North Africa and then on to Sicily and Italy; these units operated in tactical situations governed by the land campaigns. A very notable exception was the mission to Ploesti on 1st August 1943.

The extensive oil fields surrounding Ploesti were then estimated to be supplying 60 per cent of Germany's crude supply and as such constituted an extremely lucrative target for attack. This Rumanian town had been the scene of the AAF's first, if fruitless, strategic bombing mission and its importance was recognised by General Arnold who prompted plans for a new assault. As finalised, the plan involved the two B-24 groups of the 9th AF in Libya, the 98th and 376th (the latter being the descendant of the Halverson detachment that made the first raid), and three 8th AF groups.

The operation was conducted by the 9th AF which was also responsible for the tactical planning. To obtain the maximum element in surprise and give a greater chance of bombing accuracy, the unusual step was taken of training the crews to attack at very low level. Seven key installations were briefed and if all should be destroyed considerable hurt could be done to Germany's war economy. The mission entailed a round trip of 1,900 miles, the outward course being flown at medium level across the Mediterranean, over Albania and southern Yugoslavia before veering east across Bulgaria. Approaching the target area, the B-24s came down to 500 feet or less on the run up. Unfortunately the leading group, the 376th BG, turned too early for the approach to the Initial Point, and followed by another group subsequently attacked Ploesti from the wrong direction. Considerable confusion resulted with some units attacking targets not assigned to them. The prematurely alerted defences took a heavy toll of low flying Liberators; fifty-four of the 177 despatched failed to return, an exceedingly high price even if enormous damage had been done and something under half the refining capacity destroyed. As in so many instances the lasting effect was overestimated and only one month was to pass before the Germans were again operating Ploesti at pre-mission capacity.

Alpine peaks breaking a 'solid undercast' as B-24Ds of 376th BG, 15th AF wend their way towards a German target.

The surviving B-24s of the five groups were employed in another strategic mission, one originally planned in conjunction with the 8th AF strike from Britain at Regensburg but frustrated by bad weather. This was the fighter factory at Wiener Neustadt in Austria, entailing an even longer round trip than Ploesti. It was significant too as the first U.S. heavy bomber mission launched from the Mediterranean theatre (in this instance Libya) to Hitler's Reich. The bombers apparently achieved an element of surprise as only two were lost of the 114 despatched. Shortly after this mission the 8th AF contingent returned to Britain.

Establishment of the 15th AF

In the late summer of 1943 several high level policy decisions were taken affecting the deployment of the American air forces in both the European and Mediterranean theatres. With the cross-Channel invasion of continental Europe set for the following spring, there was need to build a large supporting tactical air force in the United Kingdom. To this end the 9th AF, less most of its units and personnel including the two B-24 groups then assigned to the 12th AF, was transferred from Libya to England in October.

Early in the year an Allied command, Northwest African Strategic Air Force, had been formed to embrace the operations of both RAF and USAAF heavy bombers in the theatre, the main element being the four B-17 groups which had been taken from 8th AF consignment. Despite its title, missions undertaken by this organisation were of a tactical nature in the sense that target selection was motivated by furthering the campaign to drive the enemy from Africa and then Sicily and Italy. Whether or not some targets were of tactical or strategic import was arbitrary, but in any case the bombers of the Northwest Strategic Air Force were not committed to a strategic directive. However, the possibility of basing heavy bombers in North Africa for strategic purposes had entered into USAAF planning but had been ruled out by range problems. Once southern Italy had been occupied a Mediterranean-based force could be considered.

Weather had been a major obstacle to 8th AF's pursuance of the CBO from Britain, but Italy appeared to offer more favourable conditions during the winter months. Based in Italy, heavy bombers would be within range of many targets in southern Germany and eastern Europe which were beyond the reach of the 8th AF in Britain. The factories at Wiener Neustadt and Regensburg, responsible for most of the Me109 fighters, were much more

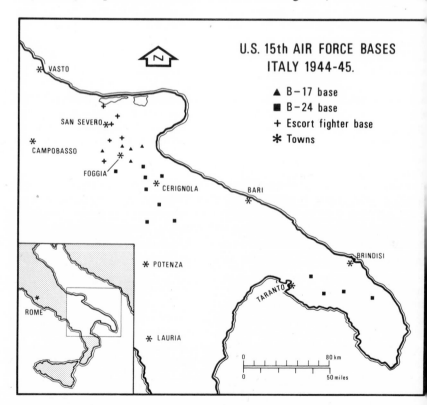

accessible from Italian bases which also provided an excellent launching place for raids on the Ploesti oil fields. These advantages prompted General Arnold to order the creation of a new strategic air force in the Mediterranean Theatre of Operations (MTO), the 15th, although not without opposition among his commanders, notably Eaker, who believed this would hinder the build-up of the 8th AF to maximum strength. There were some disadvantages: the hazard of the Alps, the poor base area facilities and it was debatable if any real weather advantage existed or, all things considered, if a higher rate of operations could be attained. Nevertheless, the 15th AF was officially established on 1st November 1943. Its first heavy bomber combat groups were the four B-17 and two B-24 from the 12th AF; the 12th AF then became the U.S. tactical air force for the theatre. The main strength of the 15th AF would be provided by diverting fifteen groups from the 8th AF's schedule – equivalent to a whole air division – these to be on hand by the end of March 1944. This would place the 8th AF with forty-one heavy groups and the 15th with twenty-one, totals that were, in fact, eventually realised.

The general base area for the 15th AF was in the plains around Foggia in south-eastern Italy, many of the actual airfield sites having been originally prepared by the Germans. Base facilities were at first generally primitive with tent accommodation and steel plank runways and dispersal points. Some accommodation was in requisitioned properties. The original six bomb groups did not move in, however, until the final weeks of the year, conducting their early operations for the 15th AF from Tunisia. The first missions, keyed to the CBO plan, were actually undertaken before the 15th AF was formed. On 1st October the B-24s, accompanied by three 8th AF Liberator groups on yet another detachment from the U.K., went back to Wiener Neustadt, while the B-17s with P-38 escort seeking another aircraft plant at Augsburg made their first mission into Germany. It was not an auspicious beginning as cloud foiled the B-17s and both forces came under concentrated fighter attack, the B-24s also encountering heavy flak; these defences claimed fourteen and damaged over fifty.

Another attempt to lay waste the Messerschmitt factory at Wiener Neustadt on 24th October was by contrast a 'milk run' but largely abortive through cloud blanketing the target. The same objective featured in the first mission flown for the 15th AF on 2nd November when 112 B-17s and B-24s were despatched – the three 8th AF B-24 groups having returned to England. This raid wrought the heaviest damage so far achieved at Weiner Neustadt with destruction of many buildings that led the Allies to assess that the Luftwaffe would be deprived of 250 fighters a month. The cost to the comparatively small task force was eleven bombers.

The promising opening shot of the 15th AF was not be be equalled until late February. During the intervening months missions were flown to strategic targets but mostly these were at short range in northern Italy, southern France or near the Balkans. Tactical missions were also undertaken in support of the Italian ground battles. Poor base facilities, inadequate fighter escort, and weather limited the scope of operations.

The 15th was formed under Major General James H. Doolittle whose command was brief, for at the end of 1943 General Arnold made a number of changes in his air force commanders in Europe. Spaatz was returned to

England to head the U.S. Strategic Air Forces in Europe (USSTAF)* a new headquarters designed to co-ordinate all USAAF activities in German war theatres and exercising overall operational control of both 8th and 15th AFs. Lieutenant General Ira Eaker moved from the 8th AF to take command of the Mediterranean Allied Air Forces (MAAF) encompassing American, British and other allied air commands in that area. Doolittle took Eaker's place as 8th AF commander and Major General Nathan F. Twining, formerly serving in the Pacific, moved to the 15th AF.

During December and January the 15th AF received its first reinforcements, six B-24 groups, fresh from the U.S.A. The B-24 predominated in the 15th AF as all but two of the fifteen groups diverted from the 8th AF would be so equipped. The 8th AF too was receiving a preponderance of B-24 groups during the winter of 1943–44 and like those reaching Italy the aircraft were chiefly the B-24H and J models featuring nose turrets. The first B-24Hs arrived in England late in August 1943 with the 392nd BG. While these aircraft were better armed the fitting of nose turrets restricted the outlook of the bombardier giving poor forward visibility, often preventing early recognition of the target and contributing to poor bombing results. A disturbing factor of the new model Liberators was that the increased weight adversely affected flying qualities when the aircraft were flown with maximum loadings, as required in most combat situations. Stability at high altitude was very poor and piloting a Liberator required far more perseverance and effort than did the B-17. In such conditions the Liberator was more likely to be wrecked through battle damage or technical emergencies than the B-17, factors contributing to a higher loss rate per sortie. Nevertheless, despite technical shortcomings of the new models, the B-24 in the hands of proficient units could equal and surpass the work of its running mate.

The Fortress had also undergone refinement resulting in the B-17G model featuring 'chin turret' frontal defence. Examples arrived in England from September 1943 as replacements and equipped all new groups arriving after November; this, too, was heavier than preceding Fortress models but flight characteristics were little changed.

New escort fighters also made their appearance during this period. Two groups of P-38 Lightnings had arrived in England during the late summer to become operational towards the year's end. Although great things were hoped for from these fighters, which were very popular in the Pacific, technical problems peculiar to the humidity and cold conditions at high altitude in Europe rendered them largely impotent. Malfunction took a far higher toll of the P-38s than the enemy during its early months of operations. Great things were also expected of the P-51B Mustangs which had shown interceptor performance combined with good endurance, in fact the P-51B on its internal supply could fly as far as the P-47 could currently reach with the aid of drop tanks. With two 75 gallon under-wing jettisonable tanks, the Mustang had a 500 mile radius of action affording escort all the way to most bomber targets. After introductory and exploratory missions in early December sufficient were available by early January to give target support as far distant as Kiel, and on the 11th of the month P-51s were instrumental

* Physically the 8th AF headquarters became USSTAF and that of VIII Bomber Command became the new 8th AF HQ.

in preventing even heavier losses to a bomber stream disorganised by weather in the Brunswick area. Initially only a single group was available, two others joining the action in February but not until the spring were anywhere near the desired number of these excellent fighters available.

In late February a brief break in the pattern of overcast skies enabled Spaatz to unleash the first co-ordinated onslaught by the 8th and 15th AFs against the German aircraft industry, a plan devised in November under the code name ARGUMENT and also involving the RAF in night attacks. While the demise of the enemy air force had long been the intermediate objective for the CBO air strikes from England, the approach of the cross-Channel invasion made it imperative that air superiority should be quickly obtained. The 8th AF P-47 groups, by now quite accomplished, had made heavy inroads into Luftwaffe fighter strength in the west. From the outset German fighters had avoided or ignored the escort and concentrated on attacking the bombers. The persistence of this tactic had enabled the experienced P-47 units to pick off the enemy fighters as they prepared to attack. Only on very rare occasions had the Luftwaffe made a positive effort to engage and disrupt the American escort, a neglect which was to cost them dear.

In view of the attrition brought to the Luftwaffe by the American fighters, the 8th AF hoped that the combined effect of harassment in the air and destruction of the planes by bombing would eventually achieve the desired results. ARGUMENT, which became known to the press as 'Big Week', commenced on 20th February when the 8th AF despatched all twenty-seven heavy bomb groups available on what was its first 1,000 bomber raid. The 15th AF was committed to support of a critical situation at Anzio and did not take part. Twelve primary targets were briefed, chiefly in the Brunswick-

Fuel aflame, an 8th AF B-24 is shot out of formation during the mission to Ludwigshafen, 7th January 1944.

Left:
Accurate strike by 305th BG B-17s on snow-highlighted fighter components plant at Leipzig/Heiterblick; a 'Big Week' mission, 20th February 1944. Note attempted smoke screen bottom left corner.

Leipzig area, the majority fighter assembly plants. Visual bombing was good with heavy damage at many places. For another five consecutive days the campaign was pressed and despite the frustrations of weather many targets were devastated. Aircraft or component factories at Steyr, Gotha, Halberstadt, Bernburg, Fürth, Augsburg, Schweinfurt and Regensburg were principal targets; Regensburg being attacked by both the 8th and 15th AFs on the 25th. Overall the bombing was good and if the Allied estimates of production loss tended, as usual, to vere to the optimistic, a considerable number of fighter aircraft had been denied the Germans at a critical time and the repercussions in shortages of parts were felt for many months. The cost was high, although not as high as USSTAF had feared. A total of 226 bombers were lost, the larger portion of 137 by the 8th AF which flew the larger number of sorties. For the four 15th AF B-17 groups the mission to Regensburg on the 25th was a disaster as this force of 176 was set upon by the Luftwaffe and thirty-three, nearly one fifth, failed to return.

In March the 8th AF made its opening strikes on a bearing factory and an engine accessories plant in the Berlin suburbs, or a rail terminus area of the city if pathfinder methods had to be used. The first attempts were generally defeated by heavy cloud but on the 6th 730 B-17s and B-24s had more success. The resultant air battles as the German fighters strove to defend their capital brought the highest loss of heavy bombers ever sustained by the 8th AF – sixty-nine. Some fell to flak but the fighters were responsible for most. Counter claims were ninety-seven destroyed by bomber gunners and eighty-two by escorting fighters, true German losses were nearly 100.

By April the 8th AF was in a position to regularly put up over 1,000 bombers for missions and the 15th AF could muster 500. The latter's attention was largely directed to targets in Italy and its ventures over the Alps into Germany were also prevented by continual weather fronts with ground screening cloud. Indeed, there appeared little if any weather benefit for the Italian-based bombers, the chief advantage of their location being the ability to reach targets in the Balkans that the 8th AF could not. Airfields were veritable mud traps in the winter deluges, making life for service personnel far more uncomfortable than in England.

With the coming of spring and steadily expanding forces, the 8th AF continued to strike at CBO objectives whenever possible but it too was frequently directed to other duties – attacks on the V-weapon sites, communications and coastal defences along the French coast. On 14th April strategic bombing forces in Europe were formally placed under the control of Supreme Headquarters Allied Expeditionary Force (SHAEF) for the cross-Channel invasion, OVERLORD. There was, however, little immediate change in target policy and the strategic air forces continued whenever possible to strike at the priority targets listed for the CBO. In any case, by the end of April it was evident that air superiority in the west had been obtained. After February there were increasingly more occasions when the Luftwaffe failed to challenge a major raid or reacted half-heartedly.

The first priority of the CBO had been achieved, but principally by the attrition of German fighter units rather than bombing attacks. The bombers, of course, were instrumental in this defeat because it was they that both baited and destroyed the German fighters. At this date Allied intelligence

A 452nd BG Fortress over Berlin during the 29th April 1944 raid. Aircraft can be seen on Templehof airfield, top left corner of picture.

still attributed more to the bombing than was achieved. Production, believed to be seriously affected, was in reality increasing, for although the heavy attacks in the opening months of 1944 had deprived the Luftwaffe of several hundred fighters, they came at a time of expanding production. In the previous spring, when the 8th AF precision attacks really began to worry the Germans, they began to increase and disperse fighter production, with the result that at the time of the USSTAF and RAF raids in February 1944 losses due to bombing were balanced by the increase in production.

Oil accorded third priority in the CBO had received scant attention from the heavy bombers since the epic Ploesti raid. The low priority was determined by the difficulty of eliminating sufficient of the numerous and widely dispersed processing plants and stores to bring about a worthwhile reduction

Interlocking pierced-steel-plank was used extensively in Italy for runways and taxi tracks. This 376th BG B-24H is under repair on an Adriatic shore after returning from operations with heavy battle damage.

Right:

Messerschmitt plant at Weiner Neustadt under attack by 15th AF B-17s. Some salvoes have over-shot target.

of petroleum production. Before the war Germany had to import two-thirds of their petroleum requirements but with the Allied blockade requirements had to come from synthetic processes using coal. Over three-quarters of total production was being obtained in this way by 1944, the remainder chiefly from Balkan oilfields of which the major centre was Ploesti. Despite the size of the task several Allied planners believed a bombing offensive would be effective; early in 1944 General Spaatz became particularly keen to follow the campaign against the Luftwaffe with one against oil.

Many Allied commanders were not convinced, notably some of the British who would have preferred a campaign against centres of transportation. In view of the opposition Spaatz initiated the operation under the pretext of furthering the aims of the CBO to suppress the Luftwaffe, as oil was vital to aircraft. To avoid the principal objectors complaining of diversion of effort, the initial missions were ostensibly against rail yards – adjoining oil refineries at Ploesti! On three occasions in April, commencing on the 5th with a force of over 200 bombers, the 15th AF struck at Ploesti with excellent results. Meanwhile the 8th AF was prepared for action against the synthetic plants. Weather and OVERLORD commitments prevented an attack until 12th May when nearly 900 heavies struck six targets at Brux, Lutzhendorf, Zwickau, Merseburg, Böhlen and Zeitz, bombing at the latter three being particularly telling. The implied purpose of this mission was to bring up the German fighters, which it certainly did, with estimates of between two and three hundred attempting interception and accounting for most of the forty-six bombers failing to return. Similar missions towards the end of May also brought stiff reaction and the German fighters frequently appeared in force to challenge the 15th AF in its regular visits to Ploesti, giving an indication of how vital these oil facilities were to the enemy.

Following the invasion of Normandy on 6th June, the 8th AF devoted its attention to tactical missions for much of the summer, including mass bombing of enemy forward positions. During June Spaatz had received top-level endorsement of his policy with oil and this became the priority for his bombers when they were not aiding the Allied armies. Incidentally, on D-Day the last USSTAF heavy bomber group became operational; this B-24 unit brought the 8th AF strength to forty-one groups operating some 2,100

bombers. Twenty-one groups flew B-17s and nineteen others B-24s while the Pathfinder group had a mixed complement. Five of the last groups joining the 3rd Division had B-24s, but between July and October these groups converted to B-17s because of the difficulty of operating two different bomber types in one command. The 15th AF's twenty-one heavy groups were made up of six with B-17s and fifteen with B-24s, totalling over 1,100 aircraft. RAF Bomber Command had a strength of about 1,500 at this date.

Russian and American soldiers watch the arrival of 97th BG B-17s after the first 15th AF 'shuttle' mission: 21st June 1944.

With a view to striking the Axis from the east, the United States persuaded the Russians to provide airfields in the Ukraine. In the event these were not used as permanent bases but as intermediary stops for formations from the 8th and 15th AFs, which could strike distant targets and then fly on to these

convenient bases in Russia. The 15th AF instigated this procedure on 2nd June when 130 B-17s accompanied by P-51s left their Italian bases to bomb a rail junction in Hungary and landed at airfields near Kiev. A mission on the 4th to attack a Rumanian airfield was flown from and back to the Russian bases, followed a week later by the bombing of another Rumanian airfield as the bombers made their return to Italy. The whole expedition had been accomplished with the loss of only two B-17s in combat. The experience of a similar sized force from the 8th AF, which flew a 'shuttle' via Berlin to the Russian bases on 21st June, was quite different. While the main force rested at their Russian base of Poltava the Luftwaffe sent its own bombers under cover of darkness to attack the field with the result that sixty-nine B-17s were disabled, forty-three of which were completely destroyed and the ammunition and fuel storages devastated. The survivors of the 8th AF force returned by way of Italy engaging in two more bombings before returning to England. The 8th AF made three similar 'shuttle' operations in August and September. The 15th AF sent no more bombers although its fighters were active in shuttles to Russia on two occasions during the summer. The practical value of these ventures appeared to wane as the Russians advanced west, besides which the Russians became increasingly unco-operative making it plain that they no longer favoured the American activity on their soil.

There were few days in the summer and early autumn of 1944 on which the 8th and 15th AF bombers were not active, although over half their bomb tonnage fell on targets of a tactical nature. Bombing accuracy steadily increased from a 20 per cent average within 1,000 feet of the aiming point to 47 per cent by mid-summer, the 15th AF doing slightly better than the 8th with approximately 50 per cent. On the other hand the loss ratio of the 15th AF was consistently higher than the 8th's, sometimes running at 30 per cent of the force despatched. The possible reasons for this are principally a less well developed escort technique and rougher terrain giving less opportunity for badly damaged bombers to return.

German anti-aircraft artillery had been improved during the latter part of 1943 and by the following spring was claiming more victims than German fighters. This trend became more pronounced as both the quality and quantity of the flak weapons improved, while Luftwaffe activity lessened. Large numbers of flak guns surrounded all major targets, particularly oil installations. The synthetic plants at Merseburg-Lunea had the heaviest flak defences; refineries near Vienna and those at Ploesti being runners up. Altitude no longer afforded the protection it had given in the past and the normal B-17 operating heights now came well within range of heavy anti-aircraft guns. Fire control systems, making use of new gun-laying radars, enabled these weapons to be used with deadlier effect.

To counter this growing opposition routes to and from targets were carefully plotted so wherever possible known flak areas could be avoided – but there was no escape at the target. Because of their better altitude performance the 8th AF often sent the B-17 divisions against the most heavily defended targets to try and mitigate losses. Smaller formations and evasive manoeuvres proved helpful too, but throughout the summer and autumn of 1944 flak losses rose, particularly at the oil targets.

Flak claimed large numbers of bombers on nearly every mission to Merse-

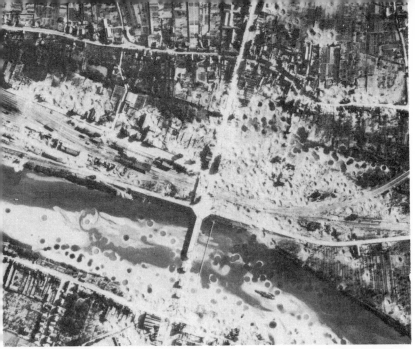

A tactical target, this bridge at Saumur, France, gives a good example of the aim and concentration achieved by a single 38-plane B-17 formation (91st and 381st BGs). The bridge has been shattered in five places and nearby rail facilities have also been pulverised: 24th June 1944.

A German attempt to screen a potential target by igniting smoke pots. On this occasion it was not the objective for these B-17s of 91st BG.

burg, culminating in the debacle of 30th November 1944 when an unexpected head wind slowed the bombers and helped the enemy gunners shoot down or cripple fifty-six B-17s. Against the enemy's gun-laying radar devices various counter measures were employed, one of the most successful being *Window*, vast quantities of metallic strips that saturated radar signals.

Despite the new dangers, the chances of survival for a bomber crewman had improved from approximately 35 per cent in early 1943 to over 70 per cent towards the end of 1944. In consequence, the arbitrary number of missions for a tour of duty was raised from twenty-five to thirty in the spring of 1944 and in the late summer to thirty-five. At this time the 8th AF had almost two crews on hand for every bomber. The 15th AF, however, did not attain this happy position until the end of the year.

Battle damage:

Above:
Cannon fire (448th BG)
Above right:
Flak burst (96th BG).
Right:
Rocket burst (100th BG).

When the ground situation allowed, both U.S. Air Forces and RAF Bomber Command returned to strategic targets with oil still priority. By mid-August the 15th AF, at the cost of 350 bombers, had all but put Ploesti out of action with some 13,400 tons of bombs. This force now turned its attention to the synthetic plants in the south and east of the Reich. These synthetic plants were cleverly structured to facilitate rebuilding or repair within a few weeks, and so neutralising them required repeated bombing. There was no doubt that this campaign had a serious effect, for there were many indications that both enemy air and ground units were often desperately short of fuel. After the first two months of attacks production was down by a half, and with the loss of Ploesti and continuing raids on crude and synthetic facilities, it was by September only a quarter of the pre-campaign rate.

In August a series of missions were flown against military vehicle factories and associated depots to further plans to prevent large-scale replacement of fighting vehicles and mechanical transport lost by the Germans in the retreat across France. Twenty-seven such targets were listed for attack and over 20,000 tons expended against those selected but the results, though often

bringing heavy destruction, did not greatly stem production. SHAEF then replaced this as the next priority to oil with the German railway system, which though frequently attacked in the past, was usually a secondary target or one of opportunity. The campaign though very heavy (the 8th AF alone dropped some 30,000 tons) was too widespread to bring about a complete stoppage on the highly developed rail system. The German Ardennes offensive, launched in mid-December, proved that the bombing had not prevented war material, including heavy armour, reaching the front.

The heavy bombers did not neglect the German aircraft industry and occasional missions to such targets were flown throughout the last half of 1944. Of concern were the new jet fighters coming into service and many strikes were aimed at production and development centres. Also it was obvious that despite supposedly crippling raids against the main sources of fighter production earlier in the year, Luftwaffe fighter strength was increasing. The Germans were dispersing the industry; the twenty-seven principal factories engaged in fighter production were scattered over 700 sites, hidden in smaller works, or camouflaged in mines, quarries and woods where they might escape the notice of Allied photographic reconnaissance. In this way production of the conventional fighter types, the Me109 and FW190, had increased from over 1,000 units in February 1944 to more than 3,000 in September, admittedly a peak for thereafter manufacture would be hit by lack of materials and power. Dispersal was not confined to this industry; bearing production and wherever practical other vital war industries were tucked away on small sites. Oil too was considered for dispersal but the complicated structures and raw material supply facilities were difficult to screen effectively.

Becoming desperately short of fuel, the Luftwaffe chose to conserve supplies for an occasional massive display of strength, when from 300 to 600 fighters took to the air to challenge the bombers. That these attempts never resulted in a mass slaughter of the bombers in one short battle, was due to the abysmally poor standard of new pilots. Few of the old hands remained and fuel shortage allowed so little flying time for tactical training that the inexperienced pilots were easily outfought by their highly trained Allied contemporaries.

In the spring of 1944 the Luftwaffe had formed special fighter units

When the Russians captured the Ploesti oil fileds they found them devastated. Damage at the Concordia Vega refinery bore witness to the effectiveness of strategic bombing.

equipped with heavily armed and armoured FW190s intended as bomber destroyers. Using a mass attack technique against isolated B-17 and B-24 formations, these units had been able to bring down whole squadrons in one pass. Undoubtedly they were the most effective means towards making the raids prohibitive, but these 'storm groups' could not be exploited due to their vulnerability to interception by Allied escorts. On the occasions when these units did reach the bombers their success showed how vulnerable the B-17s and B-24s had become on their own.

Jet fighters, encountered first in the summer of 1944, increased their activity in the autumn. With a 100 mph advance over conventional piston-engined adversaries, the Me262 posed a threat to both the strategic bombers and their escorts. This menace was thwarted due to escort fighter tactics, by attacking the jets when they were most vulnerable at landing and take-off, and using their greater manoeuvrability. Mechanical troubles also frequently left jets prey to Allied fighters. Now and then they reached the bombers, but their great speed was a handicap when it came to making accurate sighting on the lumbering B-17s and B-24s.

The surprise German offensive in the Ardennes caused the 8th AF to divert its main effort to missions that would help deflate the dangerous 'bulge' in the front. Despite a period of exceedingly foggy weather, followed by a period of icy conditions, the 8th AF despatched its largest operation of the war on Christmas Eve when 2,055 bombers set out to bomb communication centres and 'choke points' east of the battle area. In this and subsequent operations to stay the German offensive, a tremendous tonnage of bombs was put down on rail, road and canal targets with telling effect.

Meanwhile the 15th AF, continuing the air war against oil, carried out some of its most accurate bombing and completely disabled some of the plants. Oil and communications were the chief objectives for the strategic bombers in the new year, despite persistent winter cloud. Bombing was by pathfinder methods for 80 per cent of the missions during these winter months, with the 15th achieving on average twice the accuracy of the 8th AF.

The reason for the 15th's ability with radar could be traced to a better system of training and employment. Whereas the 8th had come to establish a specialist section or squadron devoted to radar bombing in every group, the 15th chose to concentrate this equipment and operators in only part of its bomber force. The 8th AF improved its radar standing in later months but overall the 15th had a much better showing with this equipment. The 8th had made good use of the G-H and Micro-H devices, both using signals transmitted by ground stations to give pin-point location and very promising blind-bombing. There were other developments in airborne radars, notably *Eagle*, a development of H2X which was undergoing operational trials near the end of hostilities.

To assist the Allied armies in their final assault on Germany, another blow at communications was scheduled under the plan called CLARION. Comprehensive in scope, CLARION called for attacks on rail, road and waterways in towns and villages not previously briefed for attack. To achieve maximum accuracy the heavies were to bomb from less than half their normal altitude, 10,000 feet. This was deemed expedient as most heavy flak areas would be avoided, and this proved so when the plan was executed on 22nd and 23rd February. In this, the largest combined Allied air strike operation over the Reich, including 1,400 8th AF and 700 bombers from the 15th; losses by enemy action were under a dozen.

The raids appeared far-reaching in their effect and while the Germans were resilient enough to keep vital services running, transportation within the Reich was gradually deteriorating. The British bombers, turning more to daylight attacks as the threat of the Luftwaffe receded, made regular incursions of the Ruhr from the autumn of 1944. The RAF had also practised precision attacks at night through new systems of target marking, and with its larger bombs could often demolish difficult targets which seemed impervious to the smaller bombs of the American air forces. Conversely, the 8th and 15th were often called upon to undertake missions against urban areas which were in part directed at breaking the resistance of the population,

A stricken 8th AF B-17 goes down in flames after a direct flak hit over Ruhland oil targets.

79

although in such missions rail and other industrial targets in the vicinity were actually briefed. General Spaatz in particular, had avoided any operations that could be misconstrued for what the Germans called terror raids, believing that the work of his strategic bombardment bombers should not be so tarnished. Unavoidably, the U.S. heavies, through spillage, error and jettisoning, caused heavy damage and loss of life in many urban areas although all attacks had planned military or industrial objectives.

While the radar aids enabled the bomber to operate in all but the worst of conditions and a non-operational day was now the exception, much of March and April 1945 were, in contrast to the previous year, blessed with many fine days. The strategic bombers went about their task in large numbers dropping great tonnages with much accuracy. Oil, jet airfields and factories, ordnance and vehicle factories and even U-boat yards were bombed and the German transport network too continued to be severely harassed. In this month there was little doubt of the overall effect of this bombardment with signs of a breakdown in the German economy. True, strategic targets were now few as the Western Allies and the Russian forces drew closer together. As a grand finale the 15th AF made its first and only attack on Berlin on 24th March, the following day flying its final strategic missions, to factories in the Prague area. Further 15th AF operations were all of a tactical nature, chiefly to aid the armies in Italy. There were strategic targets in the north of Germany for the 8th AF to attend to and in April the Luftwaffe could still make a challenge, but soon, too, this largest of all air forces found only tactical targets left. General Spaatz had notified both Doolittle and Twining on 16th April that the strategic campaign was ended.

After VE Day, 8th May, the bombers soon returned to the United States, some units to be re-equipped with B-29s for deployment in the Pacific Theatres. This was never fulfilled, although the 8th AF did transfer its headquarters to Okinawa and had received some new combat groups when hostilities ceased in August.

The Achievement of the Strategic Bomber in Europe

Without examination of the enemy's ledger there could be no doubt that air power, in all its facets, was the decisive element in the defeat of the European Axis, a fact readily acknowledged by German leaders and experts, both military and economic. Having provided three-quarters of these forces the USAAF's leaders could draw great satisfaction from the results and know that the ascendancy of the air weapon could not be challenged by the narrow views of military traditionalists. There remained, however, the vital question of what was the true contribution and value of the strategic bomber to the victory; for this above all had been the AAF's article of faith in achieving the long sought independent role for American air power. For all the trials and tribulations there was no doubt confidence among AAF commanders that strategic bombardment was omnipotent. Before the end of the war, following the 15th AF's last strategic mission, General Arnold had shown his fervour when he wrote to General Spaatz '. . . you have definitely established the strategic air force for all time to come as the spearhead of any offensive.'

Spaatz, a year earlier, had suggested to Arnold that an independent committee prepare an unbiased report on the bombing offensive. This idea had its appeal as a way of informing both government and public and would provide indisputable proof if traditionalists of other services were later to deprecate the effects of the bombing campaign. That Arnold lost no time in arranging such a report indicates the confidence among AAF leaders, even at that early date, that the report could only be highly favourable. The team that followed close in the footsteps of the conquering armies was impressive both in the qualifications of its experts and the numbers involved. They produced the copious U.S. Strategic Bombing Survey which, though it had critics and suggestions of bias, thoroughly sifted the facts and produced indisputable answers to most of the important questions.

The strategic bomber did not defeat Germany as its disciples fervently believed it could at the outset of war, yet it had without question played a decisive part. Of the bomb tonnage unloaded over the Reich by the three strategic air forces, three-quarters was in the final ten months of the war and during that period the German economy had been wrecked. Further, during those ten months the bombers had frequently been diverted to non-strategic operations so that their whole weight was not concentrated on strategic objectives as it might otherwise have been. While Germany's armies had been defeated in the field, her huge production capacity, despite previous bombing, was at its peak at the start of the major period of bombing in June 1944 yet was quite unable to sustain a war economy ten months later. The signs were that had the full weight of this huge strategic bomber force been applied at a much earlier date, victory might have been brought by bombing alone, indeed Albert Speer, Hitler's armament minister and probably the keenest brain amongst the German leaders, was convinced of this. If the build-up of the strategic bomber force had followed the time schedule outlined in AWPD-1 a more positive answer might have been obtained, although clearly this plan underestimated the resilience of the German economy and the prowess of the Luftwaffe.

The most significant contribution of the strategic bomber was the almost total elimination of Germany's petroleum supplies through attacks on refineries and synthetic plants. Not begun until April 1944, it caused serious shortages for the armed forces within a few months. Persistent bombing of the same targets thwarted German repair efforts and the physical nature of the plants was such that dispersal could not be easily or quickly achieved. By the end of war production was perhaps only 3 per cent of the pre-campaign figure. All told some 130,000 tons of bombs had been aimed at the oil industry by the U.S. bombers (70,000 by 8th AF and 60,000 by 15th AF) while RAF Bomber Command contributed 90,000 tons.

The strategic bomber also played the dominant part in wrecking the German communication system with the U.S. heavies dropping 384,000 tons (235,000 8th AF and 149,000 15th AF) of the 876,000 delivered by all Allied air forces in the last six months of hostilities. AAF commanders had looked upon these missions as tactical to assist the ground forces, yet the overall effect they had was crippling to Germany's war economy. Not until late in 1944 had a widespread and concerted bombing campaign against transport been mounted, yet by early April 1945 it had brought chaos to rail and canal systems, preventing materials and fuel reaching factories and stopping war supplies reaching the services.

The oil and communications campaigns had stricken the German economy

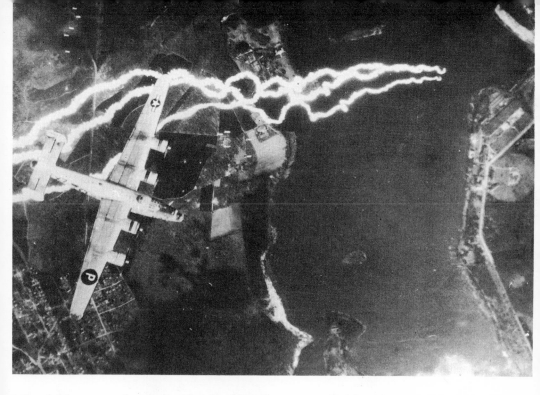

but the bombers could not have wrought this without attaining air superiority over the Reich. Destruction of the German fighter force had been the intermediate objective for the 8th AF from the early days and for a year, from spring 1943, the bombers had struck at sources of fighter aircraft production. The destruction caused was only contributing to the demise of the Luftwaffe who suffered more in the attrition of their crews in these raids. The protection afforded by U.S. long-range fighters was chiefly responsible for attaining the necessary air superiority to carry out their task. The greatest flaw in AAF plans was neglecting the need for a long-range escort fighter, through the belief that bombers could defend themselves against prohibitive losses; a fallacy the Luftwaffe was on the point of proving in the autumn of 1943, when long-range escort was at last hurried to the scene. The bombers, however, were a bait that brought the German fighters to battle, although this was certainly not in the original conception. In battles the 8th AF claimed 11,481 enemy aircraft destroyed and the 15th 3,946. Fighter claims were near to the truth but those of bomber gunners, for reasons already explained, were usually grossly inflated; on average about three out of four were false, although the actual attrition wrought by air gunners was substantial as German fighter pilots have attested.

Against the anti-friction bearing industry, a campaign associated with aircraft production, the bombers' early successes were mitigated by a failure to mount follow-up raids. Bearing production was eventually dispersed beyond serious hurt from further bombing, and the Germans were never critically embarrassed by bearing shortages. Attacks on armoured vehicle and motor transport factories brought destruction but again had no great effect on supplies to the army. The submarine campaign of 1942 and 1943

Lead bomber drops 'in train'; other aircraft in formation salvo. These are B-17Gs of 351st BG over Erfurt, 9th February 1945.

was judged a complete misdirection, for the targets were impervious to the small bombs. Nevertheless, later attacks on shipyards had brought worthwhile results. In fact, much of the success of the strategic bomber was cumulative. The enterprise and energy of Germany had shown that however hurtful a specialised bombing campaign had been it could be absorbed with time, but once the raids were of a near continuous nature expertise and resilience were overwhelmed. Examination of the instruments and weapons of the U.S. strategic bombing campaign showed that the high explosive bombs

Wreckage of the
Leuna Synthetic
Oil plant at
Merseburg

were generally too small and more incendiaries could have been used. Although the B-17 had been preferred to the B-24 for the most heavily defended targets there could be little to choose between the effectiveness of either aircraft. In the 8th AF the B-24 division led in bombing accuracy in the last months of the war.

The U.S. Strategic Bombing Survey examined other possible targets that might have been worthy of intensive bombing and concluded that the electric power system was certainly in this category. Attacks on the chemical industry and aero-engine production might also have proved rewarding. In many of the target systems attacked there was an indirect achievement. The dispersal programmes instituted by the Germans to fragment and hide vital industry from the day bombers is estimated in many cases to have caused a greater loss of production than the actual bombing.

An inestimable but considerable contribution of the strategic bomber to the Allied war effort was the tying down of over a million German military personnel in manning the air defences of the Reich and the diversion of production and development facilities to weapons and equipment and installations to mount this defence.

The cost was high: 8,314 bombers and 6,378 crews. The numbers of the recipients of the bombing who were killed is difficult to apportion but some 300,000 Germans died in air raids and about 800,000 were injured.

4. Operations: Against Japan

Heavy Bombers In Theatre Air Forces

When the Japanese made their devastating attack on Pearl Harbour on 7th December 1941, the USAAF had the equivalent of five B-17 bomber squadrons at overseas locations: one was in Hawaii and four in the Philippine Islands to where another two squadrons were in the process of moving. This deployment was to meet the threat of Japanese military activity in the south and central Pacific, with the immediate defensive intent of providing aircraft with sufficient range to carry out regular ocean surveillance. The Japanese attacks over the following weeks destroyed many of these bombers at their bases; others were shot out of the sky as they vainly tried to check the enemy offensive. Driven from the Philippines, the residue of the B-17 force then operated from Java where they were reinforced by a few early Liberators and new model Fortresses (B-17Es) brought half-way round the world. Then, as the Japanese swept through south-east Asia, this base too was denied and the survivors took up station in India and Australia to reform. Operations during this period had all been directed by the rapidly changing situation and once a static base had been reached, the meagre force of surviving high-altitude precision bombers was directed mainly, and rather unsuccessfully, against shipping.

As related, the Allies had decided to contain the Japanese while the stronger enemy, Germany, was defeated first. However, the defensive forces made available in the Pacific were sufficient to attempt the re-conquest of New Guinea, and the island strong points to the east by mid-1942. By this time the Allies were already in possession of a numerically superior air force and were progressively nearing air supremacy on all fronts. Campaigns in Pacific war theatres were mostly combined services operations involving land, sea and air forces. The part played by the heavy bombers, at first B-17s and then, from the autumn of 1943, solely B-24s, was generally a softening-up programme for enemy airfields, fortifications, stores, ports and communications, preceding each new invasion. The neutralisation of Japanese bases by-passed in the island-hopping campaigns towards Japan, was also a task for the heavy bombers. Modes of attack were eventually far removed from those in Europe with an optimum altitude of 6,000 feet for precision bombing on all targets except those defended by heavy anti-aircraft guns. Objectives were often great distances from bases and the longer ranged B-24 Liberators began to take over from the B-17 in the summer of 1942. Liberators were also employed most successfully at night against ships at sea by operating at low level and locating their targets by radar.

At peak unit strength there were 11½ B-24 bombardment groups flying against the Japanese. These were divided among the seven theatre air forces whose combined area of operations totalled some 16,000,000 square miles. The largest contingent of four groups was assigned to the 5th AF which aided the campaigns in New Guinea, then the Philippines and finally in the Ryukyus. Two groups flew with the 13th AF, which started off in the New Hebrides island group a thousand miles east of Australia and progressed through the Solomons to join the 5th AF in New Guinea and the Philippines. The 7th AF had three groups operating in the central Pacific and moving eastward through the island chains towards Japan. A single group each was the heavy bomber complement of the 10th AF in India and the 14th AF in China while two squadrons of the 11th AF kept a vigil in the bleak northern outpost of the Aleutian Islands.

While operations at this stage were basically tactical, in that they were planned to further the success of combined operations in the liberation of Japanese-held territories or to contain and tie down their forces, some strikes qualified as strategic in objective. Areas of south-east Asia rich in oil and minerals fed the Japanese war economy, notably the Dutch East Indies. Oil was always an attractive target, because its inflammable nature allowed an accurate strike by a few bombers to cause massive conflagration and considerable damage. Palembang in Sumatra, the major centre of oil production, was out of range of heavy bombers in India or Australia; but Balikpapan in east Borneo, the second most important centre in the area, was within distance of B-24s striking from Darwin, 1,300 miles away.

In May 1943 the 5th AF based a new B-24 group, the 380th BG, in the Darwin area; though its main duties were defensive with neutralising bombings of enemy outposts in the islands to the north-east of Australia, the group was occasionally given missions of strategic significance. Nickel mines in south-east Celebes was one such target that received attention but the most inviting was Balikpapan in Borneo with its busy port and large refineries. In August 1943 the group flew three small scale missions – a dozen B-24Ds was the maximum force – to Balikpapan, attacking during darkness to avoid fighter interception. While only a 2,500 lb bomb load could be carried by each aircraft, because of the extra fuel needed to make the 2,600 mile round trip, bombing caused fires and damage, although insufficient to have a prolonged effect. The Liberators were in the air for nearly 17 hours on these missions.

More than a year passed before a sizable operation could be mounted against Balikpapan, again with the handicap of extreme range. In the autumn of 1944 five missions were run by a combined 5th and 13th AF B-24 team flying out of Noenfoor Island at the north-west end of New Guinea. The flight entailed a similar long haul to that from Australia. To obtain the necessary range, armour and some equipment had to be removed from the B-24Js, which were heavier than the earlier models. Even so lightened the necessary fuel load limited each bomber to 2,500 lb of bombs. The first two strikes, on 30th September and 3rd October, were unescorted and met strong opposition. P-38 support was provided for the following missions, the fighters operating out of Morotai, 835 miles from the target. In five raids 321 B-24s bombed Balikpapan dropping 433 tons, losing twenty-two of their number. Although some of the bombing was good, the weight of the attacks was insufficient to limit production for long for, as shown in Europe, oil refinery plumbing was comparatively easy to repair. Another distant oil centre, Tarakan, 318 miles north of Balikpapan, was attacked by B-24s on 18th November and left burning fiercely. In view of the great distances involved the air forces thereafter pursued the less arduous method of denying Japan oil through the destruction of shipping.

Range was also the principal obstacle to any campaign against oil targets for heavy bombers operating from India. Chiefly employed in preventing supplies reaching the Burma front by hitting communications and ports, the 10th AF's lone B-24 group was also on occasion sent against oil targets. As early as November 1942 the 7th BG sent a handful of B-24s to bomb refineries and stores at two capital cities. Bangkok was at extreme range, nearly 1,850 miles from base, severely limiting bomb loads of the nine aircraft involved for the 16½ hour operation, longest of the war at that time. Rangoon too entailed reduced payloads for the 1,000 mile haul, but as the chief port of entry for Burma it was a worthy objective and whenever weather allowed was subject to frequent night visits from the 7th BG.

At the end of the year a theatre Strategic Air Force was created to direct operations of both British and American heavy bombers, although the overall charge was still basically tactical with the object of assisting to eject the enemy from that part of Asia. In November 1943 the 308th BG of the 14th AF joined the 7th BG in a combined series of fighter escorted day raids on targets in the Rangoon area, but the force was far too small to send against such a distant and well defended target. The 308th BG was handicapped in its operations from China by having to ferry fuel and bombs over the Himalayas before undertaking a mission, a situation that persisted until sufficient transport aircraft were available late in the war. The China based heavy bombers were predominantly concerned with aiding Chinese ground forces and striking Japanese supply routes.

The Very Heavy Bomber

From the early days of the Pacific war it was evident that the B-17 and B-24 heavy bombers would not have the range to be used strategically against Japanese war industry. Therefore the new B-29 Superfortress, doubling the radius of action of the older and smaller bombers, figured in the plans to bomb the Japanese homeland. Quantity production of the B-29 had been ordered a year before the prototype flew in September 1942; it was originally proposed that these bombers would be based in Northern Ireland and the Middle East to participate in the war against the European Axis. By the spring of 1943, as production got under way, it appeared that the B-17 and B-24 would be adequate to the task in Europe and so consideration was given to using the Superfortress in the Pacific. Even with its 1,600 mile radius of action, suitable operating bases to reach Japan could then only be found in China. Since everything going into China for the air forces had to be flown over the Himalayas, there would be a large logistic problem. An alternative was to re-capture Guam and take other islands in the Marianas group, lying 1,500 miles south-east of Japan in the central Pacific, but this would entail taking other enemy-held islands further east. By the late summer of 1943, when the first service B-29s were available for units to train to operate them, preparations were in hand to base the first very heavy bombardment wing in eastern India. There the aircraft could be more easily maintained than in China, and operations could be conducted against Japan from forward bases in eastern China.

In addition to having twice the combat radius of the B-17 and B-24, the B-29 carried three to five times the bomb load, depending on range factors, and with a maximum 20,000 lb load it grossed more than 65 tons; this was twice the weight of a war-laden Fortress or Liberator. Even at this great weight the Superfortress was a speedier bomber than the smaller contemporaries, topping 350 mph maximum when light and cruising around 220 mph when combat-loaded. It was later officially accorded the status of Very Heavy Bomber.

The armament system was highly sophisticated having four gun barbettes, aimed and fired remotely by gunners located in adjacent observation domes, and a tail gun position featuring a 20-mm cannon in addition to two 0.50-in calibre machine guns. Total defensive armament was ten 0.50s and the cannon. The crew of eleven were provided with pressurised accommodation to enhance comfort and efficiency at high altitudes, for operating up to 30,000 feet.

Early tests and development of the B-29 were very promising, in contrast to the Convair B-32 back-up design. The prototype of the latter made its first flight a fortnight before the Boeing, but was thereafter dogged with development troubles and over two years elapsed before the aircraft entered service. Slightly smaller than the B-29, the B-32 had a similar performance but only half the maximum bomb load capacity and even then less range. Such were its shortcomings that the B-32 was classified as a heavy bomber like the B-17 and B-24.

The engines used in both the new bombers were Wright R-3350 models rated at 2,200 horse-power each, near double the power of the smaller four-engine bombers. Considerable problems were experienced during the development of these engines, a situation not improved by manufacturing defects in early examples. Any aircraft, hurried into mass production, was liable to be beset with delays through technical troubles and the chief threat to B-29 acceptance was persistent difficulties with the Wright engines. The B-29 had a high wing loading and the stalling speed without flaps extended was 140 mph, thus an engine failure could be particularly critical on take-off. Initial remedial attention was directed to manufacture and assembly with better production inspection, but the failures still persisted.

During this period, when the daylight bomber campaign against Germany was ailing, even the most dedicated adherants to strategic bombing were aware that the offensive would not now defeat Germany before the Allied armies were involved in a continental invasion. In General Arnold's headquarters a new fervour was developing for what the Superfortress might achieve against Japan. With four plants building or preparing to build this sophisticated warplane and some three billion dollars invested in its production, Arnold wished to make an early showing for this expensive venture. But the modification of early B-29s to a revised combat standard threatened to delay deployment to India three to four months; this postponement displeased President Roosevelt in view of earlier assurances that the bomber would be ready for action by the end of 1943.

In December Arnold sent Brigadier General Kenneth Wolfe – who had

The 40th BG's forward base at Hsingching, near Chengtu, China, from which a B-29 required aviation spirit from 200 of these 44 gallon barrels of 100 octane to fly a mission to Japan.

supervised the B-29 establishment and training programmes and now headed XX BC (the combat agency) – to India and China to expedite arrangements in the theatre. Arnold notified Wolfe that the first B-29s would leave their Kansas training grounds on 10th March, but on arriving to see them depart was annoyed to find none ready to move. Primed by the General's wrath, a crash programme was instigated and all 150 B-29s that made up the four groups and spares contingent of the 58th BW had departed the U.S.A. by 15th April 1944.

The bombers flew via Africa to India, and at the same time a B-29 made a feint to the U.K. with the object of attracting German attention and concealing the true destination. The first aircraft reached its base near Calcutta on 2nd April but the movement from the U.S.A. was handicapped by the still undependable engines; seven B-29s crashed or crash-landed en route. An inspection revealed overheated and burnt exhaust valves and while modifications to give better cooling were effected with great urgency, flight restrictions were imposed on the B-29s. The trouble was aggravated by the high day temperatures in India; to lessen the risk of engine overheating, heavy load take-offs were restricted to between dusk and dawn.

There had been some clamour from the various theatre commanders to control the operations of the B-29s but Arnold, mindful of the diversion of effort that the strategic bombing campaign had suffered in Europe, was determined that control should be exercised from Washington, a policy endorsed by General George Marshall who headed the Joint Chiefs of Staff. Therefore it was announced that the B-29s, due to their mobility and great range, would form a truly global force not wed to any theatre. As a further safeguard Arnold took command of the air force which was created for the Superfortresses, the 20th AF, on 4th April 1944. Brigadier General

Superfortresses of 40th BG some 15,000 feet above the inhospitable terrain of northern China while on their way to attack the Anshan steel plant: September 1944.

Haywood Hansell, appointed his Chief of Staff, had much to do with the practical direction. The assignment for the 20th AF was laid down by the Joint Chiefs of Staff as '. . . the earliest possible progressive destruction and dislocation of Japanese military, industrial and economic systems and to undermine the morale of the Japanese people to a point where their capacity for war is decisively defeated.'

Arrangements had been made in November 1943 with the Chinese leader Chiang Kai-shek for the construction of five landing fields in the Chengtu area, the U.S. providing technical advisers and the Chinese the labour force. Because of the difficulty of getting construction machinery to the area, work was largely carried out by hand; each runway extending nearly two miles was made of compacted stone to support the great weight of the bombers. On 24th April 1944, Generals Wolfe and Saunders, commanding XX BC and the 58th BW respectively, took the first two B-29s over the Himalayas to the forward fields in China some 1,000 miles from the main base at Kharagpur, near Calcutta. A small fleet of transport aircraft was available to transport fuel and supplies into China, but they were quite inadequate for moving the vast quantity of fuel required to fly regular missions from China. To aid the supply situation some B-29s were stripped of armament and fitted out with extra tanks to enable them to carry 14,000 lb of fuel each from India to the Chinese bases. The first operation had been tentatively set for the beginning of May but insufficient fuel and bombs were available in China until later in the month.

The Japanese, aware of the presence of the Superfortresses, began an offensive in April 1944 aimed at denying the AAF use of air strips in the eastern provinces which had been enlarged for emergency or refuelling use by the B-29s. It seems likely that at this time the Japanese underestimated the range of the big bombers and thought the capture of the eastern airfields would forestall the American operations.

Wolfe and Saunders were finally able to despatch an introductory mission on 5th June when ninety-eight B-29s set out on a 1,130 mile flight from the Indian bases to Bangkok's rail yards. Cloud and mechanical problems hindered those attacking and bombs were scattered by instrument dropping causing little damage for the loss of five bombers. The next mission ordered was to Japan, the first American air attack on the Japanese homeland by land-based aircraft. The target was the large steel works, estimated as producing 24 per cent of the nation's total requirements at Yawata in Kyushu the southernmost island. It took two weeks to bring in the extra fuel and supplies from India and not until 13th June was all ready for the mission flown two days later. Of seventy-five B-29s scheduled, eighteen had mechanical or crew failures and one crashed on take-off. The attack was made in darkness to lessen the chance of interception. Bombing both visually and by radar was erratic and while some aircraft were damaged by anti-aircraft fire, the six bombers and fifty-five men lost were victims of mechanical failures and engine fires. This mission, the first to Japan since the Doolittle raid of April 1942, was hailed in glowing terms by the pressmen who flew in the B-29s, but the descriptions hardly matched the true results. At best the raid was a boost to Chinese morale, a blow to Japanese morale and prompted some diversion of war effort to defence of the home islands.

If Arnold was relieved to see his personal command at last engaged in its intended role, he became concerned over the inordinately slow rate of operations in the following weeks. Wolfe's bombers needed to fly twelve cargo trips each between India and Chengtu to ferry sufficient fuel, ordnance and supplies for a single mission to Japan. Heavily laden, these B-29s had to climb to the region of 20,000 feet after take-off to clear the Himalayas which strained and overheated engines, causing the loss of several aircraft. Such were the rigours of these 'Hump' trips that many crews considered them beset with more danger than combat operations. The logistic support required to maintain even fifty B-29s in China was formidable, and coupled with the high rate of unserviceability due to mechanical problems it was apparent to Wolfe and others that the transitting plans for the B-29 force were not practical. Further, it was impossible to meet operational time schedules and strengths given in directives from Washington. Arnold, apparently unhappy about Wolfe's approach to the problems, recalled him to Washington early in July to take up another command. General Laverne Saunders, a veteran of B-17 operations in the South Pacific, took over XX BC and pursued some of the objectives requested by 20th AF Headquarters.

To confuse and cause the enemy to spread his defences, attacks were planned on objectives over 3,000 miles apart. In the strategic bombing offensive against the Empire of Japan steel production was the first priority due to the greater portion being concentrated in a few large installations. One such target was at Anshan in Manchuria. The intention was to put 100 bombers over the target for a daylight precision attack, but due to the

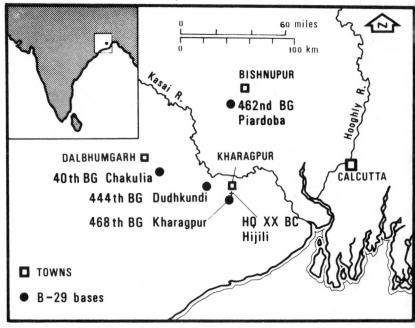

Twentieth Bomber Command in India.

familiar pattern of malfunctioning to which this time was added the miry
conditions on Chinese airfields, only sixty reached Anshan. Bombing ignited
coke and at first appeared to have wrought heavy damage, but this belief was
dispelled by the evidence of photographic reconnaissance. Only a small
percentage – perhaps $7\frac{1}{2}$ per cent of output – was judged to have been affected.
On this mission, flown 9th July, the B-29s had their first loss confirmed as
being due to enemy action, a loss somewhat overshadowed by crashes of
five aircraft through operational difficulties.

The next major mission was against the important oil centre at Palembang
in Sumatra from where an estimated 40 per cent of Japan's petroleum products were derived. AAF planners had long had designs on this inviting
strategic target. To reach this objective it was necessary to stage through an
RAF airfield in Ceylon; even so the flight was one of extreme range for the
B-29s, some 1,900 miles across the Bay of Bengal, reducing bomb loads to
only 2,000 lb per aircraft. To lessen the chance of interception, and because
the waterside location of the target would show up well on radar, the attack
was made in darkness. Part of the force dropped mines into the estuary
through which fuels and oil were shipped to Japan and the war fronts.
Flown on the night of 10th/11th August there were the usual abortives, but
of the fifty-four B-29s despatched only one aircraft failed to return – that
landing in the sea and the crew being rescued. Half the force managed to
drop over the targets as briefed, but the results were again disappointing. On
the same night a small force of B-29s operated against Japan from Chengtu
bases, raiding the aero-engine works at Nagasaki which apparently suffered
little damage.

Matters came to a head after the 20th August mission when the XX BC made its first daylight high-altitude mission to Japan to try again for the Yawata steel works. Seventy-two B-29s were greeted by the fiercest reception so far, anti-aircraft fire claiming one aircraft and three succumbing to fighters. The bombing was scattered and while the steel works took little hurt, substantial fires were started by incendiaries included in the bomb loads. Through combat damage and malfunctioning another ten B-29s failed to return, although one crew bailed out over Soviet territory. Bombers' gunners, claiming seventeen enemy fighters and many others as probables or damaged, helped to even the score but the total of fourteen B-29s lost and ninety-five crewmen dead or missing was a stunning blow.

When word reached Washington of this mission, Arnold sent Major General Curtis LeMay to take over XX BC. When commander of a pioneering 8th AF B-17 group he had contributed much to the tactics evolved. Seen by Arnold as a frank, determined leader, he had gained command of an 8th AF division.

LeMay arrived in India on 29th August and flew to Manchuria in one of the bombers launched on the next mission, another attempt at the Anshan steel works. In contrast to all the previous B-29 missions, this was a resounding success. Only fourteen of the bombers aborted and the ninety-five bombing was the highest number so far put over any target. Weather was clear and the bombing was good with damage calculated to have cut production by a third. Although the bombers were contested, only one fell to fighters, and three others to operational causes.

LeMay applied many of the lessons learned in Europe to his new command. To improve bombing accuracy he formed and trained special lead crews. For daylight raids he replaced the four-plane flight used up to that time by the staggered twelve-plane, bomb-on-leader, formation that had been evolved in the 8th AF. LeMay's efforts could still not produce the desired rate of operations or the spectacular bombing results that had been hoped for when the bombers were first sent to India. Missions from China could not be effected unless supported by a large fleet of heavy air transports to ferry in bombs and fuel.

The persistent mechanical troubles with the B-29 were gradually overcome, but the average failure rate per operation was running at 17 per cent and did not improve appreciably until February 1945. The chief obstacle to bombing accuracy was the weather which deteriorated as winter neared. As over Europe cloud confounded, yet on several occasions poor bombing was due to near hurricane force winds that buffeted, speeded or retarded, the B-29s on their target approach. Nevertheless, LeMay was able to make a dramatic improvement in getting scheduled numbers airborne for a mission and in improving the accuracy of attacks.

Strategic Operations from the Marianas

By the autumn of 1944 General Arnold accepted that little could be done to further XX BC's offensive while the logistics obstacle remained. At this juncture his attention turned to the initial operations of a second Superfortress task force. A year earlier, military leaders in Washington had shown interest in the use of the Marianas Islands, as base for B-29 operations against Japan, the great advantage being a direct sea supply lane

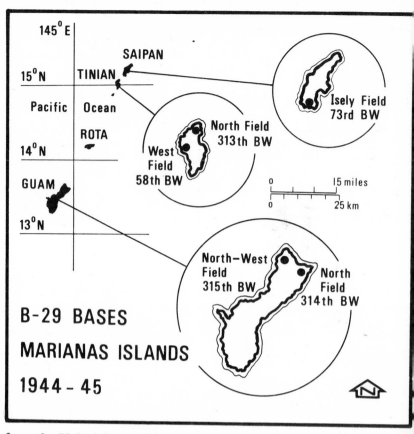

from the United States. The Joint Chiefs of Staff eventually approved a
plan to capture keypoints in the Marshall Islands which would clear the way
for an invasion of Saipan, Guam and Tinian in the southern Marianas.
Saipan was invaded by Marines in mid-June and captured after three weeks
of intense fighting; Guam and Tinian, assaulted a month later, were under
American control by 9th August. Such was the pressure from Washington to
establish a bomber airfield, work began enlarging a former Japanese Saipan
airstrip nine days after the initial landings while fighting was still in progress.

A second B-29 wing, the 73rd, training in Kansas and Colorado and originally intended to follow the 58th BW to India, was held back and redirected
to Saipan where airfield construction rapidly advanced during August and
September. Another bomber command, the XXI, was formed within 20th
AF. To lead it Arnold selected Brigadier General Haywood Hansell who had
played a notable part in the plans and direction of the AAF's strategic bombardment campaigns; lately as Chief of Staff of the 20th AF he had been
much concerned with the direction of XX BC and target priorities for bombing Japan out of the war.

General Hansell in the first B-29 to reach the Marianas on 12th October
1944 made exploratory missions before the full complement arrived at
Saipan. These were against the by-passed Japanese submarine base at Truk
Island, 630 miles south-east of the Marianas, and an airstrip on Iwo Jima,

Fractures of scanning domes caused several 'suck outs' from resulting decompression. Gunners went too: Sergeant Krantz of the 497th BG (the blob below the scanning port) was lucky in that a safety strap held and other crew members were able to pull him back into 'American Maid'.

Brigadier General Emmett O'Donnell, CO 73rd BW, talks with pilot, Major Robert K. Morgan, prior to boarding B-29 'Dauntless Dotty' of 497th BG for the first mission to Tokyo; 24th November 1944. Morgan had previously flown B-17s with the 8th AF.

00 miles to the north of Saipan from where enemy aircraft had started naking hit and run attacks against the B-29 airfield. In the first six missions, not unexpectedly, mechanical and crew problems were experienced and bombing was generally poor.

In contrast to deployment in India, where each bomb group had a sepa-ate airfield, all four groups of the 73rd BW on Saipan were concentrated on one airfield (at first only one 7,000 foot runway was available). This argely of necessity as the number of airfields that could be constructed in the

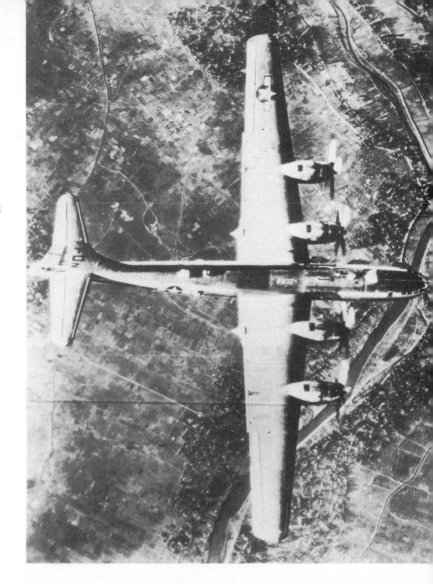

A 498th BG B-29, appropriately nicknamed 'The Heat's On', photographed 25,000 feet above the Tama River, west of Tokyo during target approach. This bomber was lost in December 1944, a victim of mechanical failure.

Marianas was limited, and partly a move to ease the logistic problems of sustaining the force. With all 150 aircraft (subsequently raised to 180 in each wing including thirty-six spares) and 9,000 men – combat and support concentrated around the Wing headquarters, maintenance and operational control was greatly facilitated. At the time of the 73rd BW's arrival on Saipan the organisation of B-29 groups was simplified by reducing the number of squadrons from four to three while increasing each squadron's aircraft complement from seven to ten.

By mid-November most of the 73rd BW had arrived and Hansell prepared his inaugural mission to Japan. The Japanese capital was an obvious choice, and in view of the increasing fighter opposition the particular objective chosen was the Nakajima aircraft engine works. Bad weather delayed the launch but eventually, on 24th November, 110 B-29s set out led by the 73rd's Commander – Brigadier General O'Donnell. Cloud hid much of the

One of seven B-29s destroyed or damaged beyond repair in a surprise straffing raid by seventeen Japanese 'Zeke' fighters on the 73rd BW's base; 27th November 1944.

Preparing M64 500 lb GP bombs for loading into the twin bays of a B-29 at Isley Field. Bomb loads were increased from 2.6 tons per aircraft in November 1944 to 7.4 tons per aircraft by August 1945 through weight economies and better operational tactics.

Tokyo area and few of the eighty-eight bombers that bombed were able to sight on the target although it was hit. Three days later Hansell sent a slightly smaller force back to the same target, but again cloud thwarted their efforts. On 3rd December a third attempt was made, this time in clear weather, but from 27,000 feet the aim of the bombers was poor and persistent fighter interception was chiefly responsible for the loss of six B-29s. The first really effective precision bombing by XXI BC came on 13th December when seventy-one B-29s hit the giant Mitsubishi aircraft and engine factory at Nagoya causing substantial damage and reducing production by 25 per cent. Five days later the Superfortresses went back to hit another section of the Mitsubishi plant only to be foiled by cloud, even so radar bombing brought damage to factory buildings although not to vital machine tools. On 22nd December a third attempt was made to put the plant out of action, this time using incendiaries. Cloud forced a radar release and the bombs were widely scattered.

In XXI BC's first two months of operations Hansell had to contend with many of the problems that had bedevilled XX BC. The weather proved worse than in Europe; persistent high winds sometimes reached over 150 mph complicating navigation and bombing precision. The Command, averaging a mission every four days, was only marginally better than XX BC during the same period. One third of the aircraft despatched had to turn back through mechanical failure while only 14 per cent hit the primary target. Hansell strove to improve the skill of his bombardiers and lead crews, who appeared to be too eager to resort to radar when conditions were unfavourable. One hindrance to bombing was restricted vision through iced-up windows necessitating new heating devices. The turn-backs were chiefly caused by engine strain due to the high loadings. Hansell had his engineer remove auxiliary bomb bay tanks and equipment considered unnecessary resulting in the saving of some 6,000 lb on each aircraft. Thus lightened, an improvement in engine reliability was evident.

Though dissatisfied with the early performance of his Command, Hansell tended to consider this an experimental period. Not so Arnold, who was no doubt apprehensive of the Joint Chiefs of Staff view if the expensive programme did not soon produce tangible evidence of success. The war in Europe might soon be concluded when the full weight of Allied power would be shifted to the Pacific with an invasion of the Japanese home islands. If the B-29s were to make this unnecessary by bombing Japan into submission, there was need of immediate improvement.

The Fire Raids

In November Arnold and Major General Lauris Norstad (Hansell's successor as 20th AF Chief of Staff) had studied a report prepared by economic experts on the vulnerability of Japan's industrial communities. War industries were concentrated in the country's largest cities – Tokyo, Osaka Nagoya and Kobe – and chiefly located in areas with a high density of dwellings and other buildings constructed chiefly of wood. Many hundreds of small businesses sub-contracted war work, these so-called home industries being widely dispersed in these combustible localities. The report, advocating the use of incendiaries against these areas, estimated their effect on the enemy's war economy would, ton for ton, be five times greater than precision bombing of selected targets. This was advocating area bombing, which the AAF had disdained to practice, and had as far as possible avoided, in Europe.

Contrary as this practice was to all previous endeavours of U.S. strategic bombing, in the light of the largely unfruitful campaign of precision attack with the B-29s, 20th AF HQ decided to explore the effect of fire raids. In mid-December Hansell was directed to launch a full-scale incendiary attack on an industrial community area with the deliberate intent of causing wholesale destruction by fire. Burning out Japanese cities did not appeal to the XXI BC leader, a dedicated advocate of precision attack on selected industrial targets, and he appears to have been unhappy after an assurance from Norstad that this was purely an experimental project. The experimental fire mission was flown on 3rd January 1945 against Nagoya. This time the incendiaries were not aimed at the Mitsubishi plant but at a section of the city which it was hoped would burn and destroy or badly damage many small

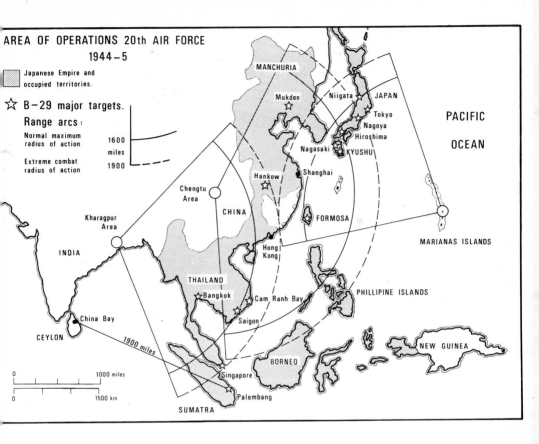

AREA OF OPERATIONS 20th AIR FORCE
1944-5

Japanese Empire and occupied territories.

☆ B-29 major targets.

Range arcs:

Normal maximum radius of action — 1600 miles

Extreme combat radius of action — 1900

MANCHURIA

Mukden ☆

Niigata

JAPAN

Tokyo
Nagoya
Hiroshima

Nagasaki ☆ KYUSHU

Hankow ☆

Shanghai

Chengtu Area

CHINA

FORMOSA

Kharagpur Area

INDIA

THAILAND
☆ Bangkok

Hong Kong

☆ Cam Ranh Bay

Saigon

PHILLIPINE ISLANDS

China Bay

CEYLON

1900 miles

☆ Singapore

Palembang

SUMATRA

BORNEO

PACIFIC
OCEAN

MARIANAS ISLANDS

NEW GUINEA

0   1000 miles

0   1500 km

factories. The results were adjudged inconclusive for, although there were many large fires and a textile mill was destroyed, the bomb pattern was not sufficiently large or concentrated to bring about a major conflagration.

At this juncture, however, Arnold decided to change his B-29 commanders, ordering Hansell back to the United States and transferring LeMay from India to take over XXI BC. The underlying reason appears to have been the growing impatience with Hansell's endeavours to achieve the aims of the 20th AF by visual precision bombardment. In LeMay a more flexible approach was recognised. In fairness Hansell, like Wolfe and Saunders before him, had little opportunity to divert from established doctrine while beset with serious technical and operational problems of the big bombers. Hansell's efforts received some vindication in the last mission he despatched prior to LeMay's arrival. In clear weather on 19th January sixty-two B-29s each unloaded 5,000 lb of ordnance over the Kawasaki aircraft factory at Akashi, near Kobe, wrecking most production facilities and all but bringing the plant to a standstill. This was without question the most successful B-29 high-altitude precision attack so far.

As he had done when taking over XX BC, LeMay made no immediate significant changes in tactics. After two high-altitude raids, the second marked by the strongest fighter opposition so far encountered, Norstad directed LeMay to carry out another exploratory incendiary raid against an industrial area. This was flown on 4th February against Kobe and the results, considerably better than those of the Nagoya raid, caused exten sive fire damage to many parts of the city. On this occasion the 73rd BW force had been accompanied by some aircraft of the 313th BW, the second B-29 wing to reach the Marianas and based on Tinian. Reconnaissance photographs revealed damage to many industrial sites and prompted 20th AF planners to give incendiary raids priority. Accordingly LeMay was directed on 19th February to begin such a campaign against the principal Japanese industrial cities.

Another high-level incendiary mission was flown against Tokyo on the 25th, and the debut of a third B-29 wing, the 314th flying out of Guam boosted the strike force to a record 229 bombers. Cloud hid the target area but subsequent reconnaissance revealed a square mile of the city burnt out There followed a high-altitude precision attack against an aircraft plant in Tokyo on 4th March which, hampered by weather, produced poor results This mission was the last prior to the change in tactics.

During the period since the first mission on 24th November, twenty strikes had been mounted against targets in Japan by XXI BC. Of these sixteen had been directed at the aircraft industry and three against the urban areas of Tokyo, Nagoya and Kobe, and one night raid against Tokyo dock region The Japanese aircraft industry was concentrated in a score of factories and 91 per cent of aero-engines were made in only three plants. Although an ideal target system for elimination the attacks carried out had, with one exception, failed to produce the expected results. The three high-level incendiary raids had been partially effective, but fires were too widely dis persed through lack of concentration and weight in the attacks.

LeMay and his staff realised that the required accuracy and concentration could be achieved by attacking from lower altitude. To avoid losses this was best carried out in darkness, since the Japanese had not offered serious opposition to night raids. Assuming that their night fighter force could be discounted, the principal danger was from anti-aircraft artillery. A reduction in altitude, avoiding climbs to 25,000 feet or higher, would also place less strain on engines and allow fuel reductions enabling a larger payload to be carried. In view of the weak opposition expected, this could be further exploited by the removal of all armament, ammunition and gunners, except in the tail position. There were other advantages. The 120 to 180 knot winds at miles high that had caused drift on target approaches and brought inaccurate bombing, were not met at lower levels.

The principal objection was the hazard of anti-aircraft fire at lower altitudes which might bring prohibitive losses. LeMay took that risk and decided to use the B-29s at between 5,000 to 6,000 feet, reasoning that it was beyond range of Japanese light anti-aircraft guns, while the large weapons might well have laying difficulties for such relatively low altitudes. Using the B-29 force in this manner would be ideal for the fire raids that now had priority. LeMay already had some experience of the advantages of carrying out incendiary strikes at lower altitude. In November 1944, while command-ing XX BC, he had been ordered to assist the theatre command in China by mounting a B-29 attack on Hankow. Through this great inland port on the Yangtse passed much of the war supplies for Japanese armies in that part of China. General Channault, commanding the 14th AF, influenced LeMay

Beyond the gunner and his computing sight in the port scanning dome, another 330th BG, 314th BW B-29 flies with radome partly extended on approach to Japan.

Framed by wreckage of Japanese aircraft, a B-29 of 505th BG, 313th BW, stands on its dispersal point at North Field, Tinian, February 1945.

in making maximum use of incendiaries and in attacking from a lower than normal altitude to improve accuracy. On 18th December the eighty-four B-29s involved dropped 511 tons of bombs, some four-fifths of which were incendiaries, from heights around 20,000 feet. Huge fires were started among the closely packed wooden buildings along the Hankow waterfront and many of these were still burning three days later. The damage and destruction to stores and port facilities were enormous.

The XXI BC's first low-altitude fire raid was flown on the night of 9th–10th March against a twelve square mile industrial community area of Tokyo. LeMay despatched 325 B-29s from the three wings, each able to average a 12,000 lb bomb load due to the weight savings. Weather was good and 279 of the bombers unloaded 1,665 tons of petroleum-based incendiaries. Fierce fires taking hold in the north-east section of the area, fanned by 20 mph winds, precipitated a holocaust. By the following mid-day an area of 15.8 square miles was almost completely burned out and over a million people – one seventh of the capital's population – were made homeless. Japanese records show that 83,783 people were killed and over 100,000 injured in the raid, higher casualties than for either of the two atomic bombs. Reconnaissance revealed a score of large factories destroyed or damaged and total disruption of public services. This staggering raid, bringing destruction on an unprecedented scale, rocked the Japanese nation; public morale never recovered.

For the 20th AF the raid had given a new direction to the course of strategic bombardment. The fears of heavy loss proved unfounded, for the defences were weak and anti-aircraft fire largely ineffective. Nevertheless, fourteen bombers failed to return although five crews were rescued from the sea. Aircraft had been despatched singly on the mission and collisions probably accounted for some of the losses.

Two nights later the same tactics were used by 310 B-29s against Nagoya and two nights after that by a similarly sized force against Osaka. At Nagoya the fires did not develop as at Tokyo, but some two square miles were burned out. At Osaka 8.1 square miles lay charred by dawn and many industries were wrecked. Kobe was the next recipient of this awesome technique of destruction with 3 square miles incinerated and on 19th March XXI BC returned to Nagoya and added another 3 square miles of devastation. Thereafter, no more incendiary raids could be run for three weeks as bomb stocks were depleted; XXI BC meanwhile pursued industrial and military objectives with mostly high explosive loads. The five incendiary missions had eliminated a total of 31.81 square miles of Japan's four major industrial areas, causing incalculable economic hurt and casualties estimated at near 220,000. American losses had amounted to 1.3 per cent of aircraft despatched.

While many AAF leaders disapproved of area bombing or attacks involving the civilian population, there was no denying that such destruction had a devastating effect on the enemy's war economy. Many western observers did not believe it was in the Japanese character to surrender, and that an invasion of the home islands would be necessary to obtain victory. Such a venture was expected to cost half a million Allied lives, to say nothing of the casualties Japan would incur, and so to many American leaders the onslaught of XXI BC was justified if it could force a surrender before the proposed invasion.

In April a new directive from 20th AF HQ required strikes both against specific industrial targets and area fire raids on industrial communities. A second low-altitude incendiary campaign was proposed against the four cities previously attacked and three others considered highly vulnerable to this technique. With replenished incendiary stocks, two such raids were launched in mid-April against Tokyo and cities in the Tokyo Bay area and, when further incendiaries were available a month later, against Nagoya and two more successive strikes on Tokyo districts. The latter were noticeable for the desperate enemy efforts to defend their capital, resulting in seventeen B-29s failing to return on the first night and twenty-six – worst loss on any B-29 raid – on the second. A total of 169 B-29s were damaged in these two operations. This second series of fire raids wrought further havoc

102

M47A2 jellied
petroleum
incendiaries fall
towards the already
fiercely burning
dock area of Kobe,
Japan's sixth
largest city: 4th
June 1945.

Identification Numbers
of Urban Areas on Map

Figures after each name indicate:
First, the total square miles of built-up
area: Second, the percentage of
that built-up area destroyed by
20th AF bombing.

1.	Aomori	2.08 – 35	24.	Hamamatsu	4.24 – 70	47.	Kochi	1.90 – 48
2.	Sendai	4.53 – 27	25.	Shizuoka	3.46 – 66	48.	Imabari	0.97 – 76
3.	Nagaoka	2.03 – 66	26.	Shimizu	1.41 – 52	49.	Matsuyama	1.67 – 73
4.	Hitachi	1.38 – 78	27.	Namazu	1.40 – 90	50.	Kure	3.26 – 40
5.	Utsunomiya	2.75 – 34	28.	Hiratsuka	2.35 – 44	51.	Hiroshima	6.90 – 69
6.	Mito	2.60 – 65	29.	Yokohama	20.20 – 44	52.	Tokuyama	1.27 – 54
7.	Toyama	1.88 – 100	30.	Nagoya	39.70 – 31	53.	Ube	1.80 – 23
8.	Maebashi	2.34 – 42	31.	Kuwana	0.82 – 77	54.	Shimonoseki	1.42 – 36
9.	Kumagaya	0.60 – 45	32.	Yokkaichi	3.51 – 35	55.	Moji	1.12 – 27
10.	Isezaki	1.00 – 17	33.	Tsu	1.47 – 81	56.	Yawata	5.78 – 21
11.	Kofu	2.00 – 15	34.	Ujiyamada	0.93 – 39	57.	Fukuoka	6.56 – 22
12.	Hachioji	1.40 – 80	35.	Wakayama	4.00 – 53	58.	Oita	2.20 – 25
13.	Kawasaki	11.30 – 33	36.	Nishinomiya	9.46 – 37	59.	Uwajima	1.00 – 52
14.	Tokyo	110.80 – 50	37.	Sakai	2.32 – 44	60.	Sasebo	2.34 – 42
15.	Chiba	1.98 – 43	38.	Osaka	59.80 – 26	61.	Saga	1.20 – 44
16.	Choshi	1.12 – 43	39.	Amagasaki	6.90 – 11	62.	Omuta	5.37 – 43
17.	Fukui	1.90 – 85	40.	Kobe	15.70 – 56	63.	Kumamoto	4.80 – 21
18.	Tsuruga	1.13 – 68	41.	Akashi	1.42 – 64	64.	Omura	5.37 – 43
19.	Ogaki	1.20 – 40	42.	Himeji	1.92 – 72	65.	Nagasaki	3.30 – 44
20.	Gifu	2.60 – 74	43.	Okayama	3.38 – 63	66.	Nobeoka	1.43 – 36
21.	Ichinomiya	1.28 – 76	44.	Fukuyama	1.20 – 73	67.	Miyazaki	0.50 – 26
22.	Okazaki	0.95 – 68	45.	Takamatsu	1.80 – 78	68.	Miyakonojo	0.50 – 26
23.	Toyohashi	3.30 – 52	46.	Tokushima	2.30 – 74	69.	Kagoshima	4.87 – 44

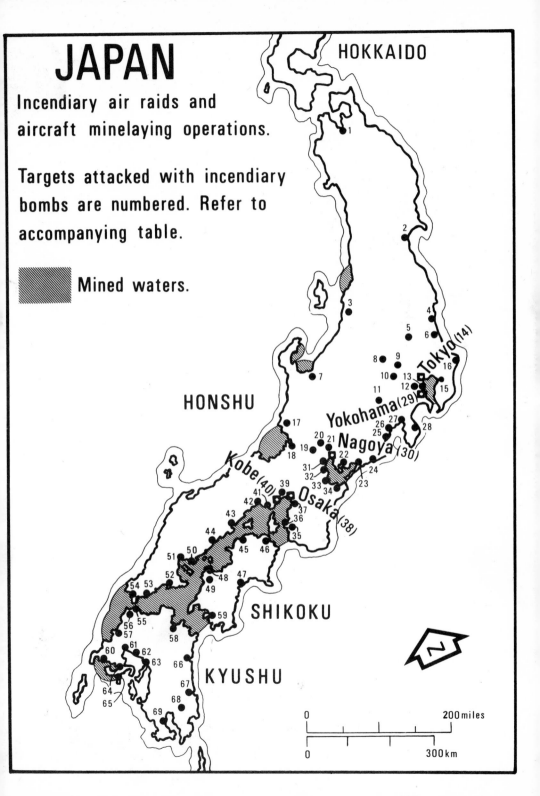

JAPAN

Incendiary air raids and
aircraft minelaying operations.

Targets attacked with incendiary
bombs are numbered. Refer to
accompanying table.

Mined waters.

HOKKAIDO

HONSHU

Tokyo(14)

Yokohama(29)

Nagoya(30)

Kobe(40)

Osaka(38)

SHIKOKU

KYUSHU

0   200 miles

0   300 km

A flight of 19th BG bombers against a backdrop of Fujiyama.

and in the six cities attacked 105.6 square miles had been charred, two-fifths of their total areas.

In mid-June XXI BC began a low-level fire campaign against the secondary cities of Japan, chiefly those with populations of between one and two hundred thousand people. There were fifty-eight in this category and during the next two months 72.5 square miles of burned out urban districts were added to the total. Japanese opposition to most raids was then so insignificant that LeMay began to announce his fire targets in advance, warning the people to evacuate the area. On 27th July 660,000 pamphlets were dropped on eleven cities warning of their impending annihilation. The following night six of these were bombed; casualties were much reduced through the inhabitants having heeded the warning and fled the localities. At this stage the Japanese people had more faith in their enemy's warning than their Government's ability to protect them.

Precision Attacks

While urban area incendiary raids were the major pursuit of the B-29s during the period March-April 1945, these operations were interspersed with attacks on specified industrial and military targets. Many were situated away from well developed urban areas and therefore immune from fire spread, or could best be destroyed by high explosives.

The success of the low/medium altitude night incendiary raids prompted a series of missions in late March and early April when attempts were made to carry out precision bombing from similar altitudes during darkness. Pathfinder methods were used with flare illumination and incendiary markers but all attacks, against aircraft component plants, proved fruitless. Target marker devices were inadequate, bombsights unsuitable and bombardiers lacked training in this technique.

106

LeMay then returned to daylight operations and, as anti-aircraft fire had proved less effective at some targets than anticipated, reduced bombing altitudes from the usual 25,000 feet to under 20,000 feet with the aim of obtaining greater accuracy. The first of these missions was flown on 7th April when the giant Mitsubishi aero-engine plant at Nagoya was finished off with a devastatingly accurate precision attack by 153 B-29s. Some bombing was from 12,000 feet at the Nakajima works, also hit this day and completely wrecked in a follow-up raid five days later. By the end of April most of the major aircraft engine plants had been heavily and effectively bombed.

During April XXI BC had also turned its attention to enemy airfields in Kyushu, denying their use to Japanese air units contesting the invasion of Okinawa, an important island in the Ryukyu chain only 325 miles from Kyushu. In February U.S. Marines had captured the island of Iwo Jima after a particularly costly battle, thus removing the menace of Japanese air raids on Saipan in which several B-29s had been destroyed in past months. Iwo Jima, lying about one thousand miles from Japan and 600 from Saipan, offered a haven for B-29s in difficulties. It was also near enough to Japan to enable fighter groups, based on its dusty strips, to support the B-29s over their targets. Later Okinawa would provide an even better location for fighters. To aid in keeping Japanese naval forces from interfering with the landings in Okinawa, B-29 support was requested in mine-laying operations to blockade enemy ports. The 313th BW assigned this task dropped over a thousand tons of mines at the entrances to the Shimonoseki Straits in four nights prior to the initial landings on 1st April, virtually closing the sea lanes in the confined waters to large ships for nearly two weeks. The Wing continued to be employed on mining throughout the spring of 1945.

With the capture of Iwo Jima the Mariannas were safe from air attack and B-29s could be closely parked to aid servicing. This is the parking area of the 58th BW at North West Field, Tinian. *Larry Griffin*

The artist has an admiring audience for his embellishment of 479th BG's 'Jokers Wild'. This aircraft has the later four-gun upper turret.

Japanese heavy anti-aircraft artillery was nowhere as formidable as that of Germany. This abandoned example still reposed on the former Japanese airstrip on Saipan a year after the island was taken.

April 1945 was also significant in that the 20th AF reached its planned strength. During the month 58th BW transferred to the Marianas from India and XX BC disbanded. They had devoted attention chiefly to south-east Asian targets during the winter of 1944–1945, ranging from Formosa to Singapore. Another B-29 wing, the 315th, arrived from the United States giving XXI BC a complement of five and over 700 very heavy bombers. With this force LeMay was able to spread his attacks over 24 hours and vary altitudes from 6,000 to 20,000 feet depending on the known defences in the areas of operation. With reduced altitudes bombing accuracy improved appreciably from 15 per cent of hits within 2,000 feet of the aiming point before this change to 26 per cent by late spring. Better lead crew training begun in the winter was also instrumental in this improvement.

A general weakening of fighter opposition was evident in the spring and allowed more diverse operations in daylight. Enemy fighter strength in the Japanese home islands was estimated as a thousand aircraft at that time. Interceptions on day raids were relatively few after June and fuel shortages further weakened fighter defences. Japanese tactics, too, were generally ill-conceived and poorly executed with individual head-on approaches predominating. Except when a vital part was struck, the armament of Japanese fighters was insufficiently heavy to destroy a large aircraft like a B-29 in a fleeting pass. Enemy pilots were, nonetheless, tenacious in their attempts to bring down the bombers and frequently resorted to ramming tactics.

XX BC continued intermittent precision attacks on the Japanese aircraft industry during May and June with the object of preventing any expansion of the home defence fighter force. In May a campaign was begun against Japan's petroleum industry with strikes on installations at Tokuyama and Oshima on the 10th. Results were excellent with almost the total destruction of the latter. Thereafter oil targets occupied the newly arrived 315th BW, based on Guam.

The 315th's aircraft were chiefly B-29B models of reduced weight equipped with Eagle radar, a sophisticated development of H2X that gave a vastly improved scope picture. These Superfortresses also had all forward turrets removed, retaining only their tail armament. The weight reductions and low-level operations enabled an average 18,000 lb load to be carried by each B-29B and on one occasion this was raised to a record 22,800 lb. Commanded by Brigadier General Frank Armstrong, one of the AAF's most experienced bombardment officers who had headed 8th AF's first B-17 group, the Wing was specially trained to operate at night employing Pathfinder techniques. Commencing these operations on 26th June the Wing completely destroyed nine principal oil refining and storage plants in fifteen missions, depriving Japan of an estimated 6,055,000 barrels of storage tank capacity. A synthetic works at Ube was not only demolished, it was submerged when bombs broke dykes protecting the reclaimed land on which it was built. The 315th BW's targets were of areas of less than 0.6 of a square mile and aircraft bombed individually. Radar was used almost exclusively, the proximity of many plants to the sea or rivers aiding accuracy. Only one B-29 from the Wing was lost to enemy action.

The 313th BW's specialist mine-laying activities continued during the summer months bringing considerable reward. Viewed with concern by

The burned out shell of the giant Mitsubishi aircraft engine plant at Nagoya.

some AAF leaders as a diversion of effort, mine-laying proved to be of great strategic value. Japan was dependent on imports to the extent of 88 per cent of all iron; 80 per cent of all oil; 24 per cent of coal; 90 per cent of coking coal and 20 per cent of food. To reduce these commodities nearly 13,000 mines were sown in the approaches to major ports, using accoustic and magnetic types in suitable waters. So telling was this campaign that by July mines were destroying more shipping than U.S. submarines, hitherto the most successful weapon in this respect.

After the defeat of Germany General Arnold had reorganised his Pacific air forces for the final assault on Japan. On 16th July he relinquished command of the 20th AF to LeMay; in effect XXI BC was redesignated 20th AF. On the same date Spaatz was appointed overall commander of strategic bomber forces operating against Japan.

Throughout the spring and summer of 1945 the pace of 20th AF operations had steadily increased with an average of a mission every other day by July and a record 6,697 sorties in that month when over 43,000 tons of bombs were dropped. Overall accuracy was good despite 75 per cent of the bombs being released on radar guidance. By early August the combined area and precision attacks had put out of action or seriously impaired production at all twenty-three major aircraft factories, the six principal munitions arsenals, two tetra-ethyl lead plants, two large steel works and the petroleum industry. Additionally 540 other factories engaged in war production had been eliminated or severely damaged, as were thousands of small machine tool and manufacturing home industry plants in urban areas. The laying waste of cities had brought a sharp decline in Japanese morale and much of the population had moved away from urban districts to escape the bombing.

110

thus creating shortages of labour and further hampering the economy. With little fuel, main war industries in ruins and many of her people near starvation, by early August Japan was a beaten nation.

The Atomic Bombs

On 6th August 1945 the status of the strategic bomber as an instrument of destruction dramatically increased. As the only practical vehicle for delivery of the atomic bombs it became the prime factor in military power. On that day the city of Hiroshima was obliterated by an atomic explosion, causing 129,000 casualties including 78,000 deaths. Over 70,000 buildings were destroyed or wrecked and 176,000 people made homeless. This holocaust caused by the single 9,000 lb missile delivered by a lone B-29 was equivalent in power to the average conventional bomb loads of 2,000 B-29s and as such was the most destructive weapon ever unleashed.

The atomic weapon had been developed in great secrecy and few people knew of its existence until the Hiroshima burst. In September 1944 a special B-29 unit was organised to deliver the bomb, the 509th Composite Group, which had a single bombardment squadron and a cargo aircraft unit for support. The commander, Colonel Paul Tibbetts, was the only man in the unit who knew the exact purpose of the unit's existence, indeed the crew of the B-29 that dropped the bomb were not informed until shortly before the first mission.

The 509th CG moved to Tinian in May 1945 and flew a number of simulated single-plane sorties using high explosive bombs. The atomic bomb programme was still then a questionable project, until proven by a test detonation in the New Mexico desert in July. Only two bombs were available for operational use by early August, the uranium core weapon used at Hiroshima and a slightly heavier plutonium core type. The decision to use the bombs was taken by President Truman and his advisers with the primary object of bringing an early end to hostilities.

Unaware of any surrender approaches – although the Japanese Government was seriously considering the matter – the second weapon was made ready for use. On 9th August, the day following Russia's declaration of war on Japan, this bomb was dropped. The primary target was Kokura but cloud and smoke concealed the aiming point, thus the B-29 involved turned for the secondary target, Nagasaki, 95 miles away. Here too there was considerable cloud but at the last moment the bombardier was able to see his target clearly. If destruction and loss of life were not as epoch making as at Hiroshima they were terrible enough to hurry a Japanese surrender. Casualties amounted to 95,000 of which 35,000 were deaths. Even this event did not bring an immediate surrender response from the Japanese Government and conventional B-29 bombing missions continued.

On 14th August 809 B-29s, the largest number ever despatched in 24 hours, attacked various industrial, military and urban targets. It was, however, on this day that Japan notified full acceptance of Allied terms. The 20th AF was about to be joined in the assault on Japan by the 8th AF, recently redeployed from the U.K. B-29 groups assigned to the 8th AF on Okinawa were preparing to fly their first operations next day and had the war lasted into the winter of 1945–46 another 1,000 B-29s were to have operated with this famous force.

The Achievement of the Strategic Bomber in the Pacific

Japan's unconditional surrender, the termination of World War II, was significant in that for the first time in the history of warfare a major power was forced into submission without armies invading its homeland. For General Arnold and the AAF HQ this was without question vindication of the long cherished belief in the validity of strategic bombardment. Other military leaders might argue, as some did, that Japan would have been beaten without bombing the homeland or the use of the atomic weapons, these only expediting an early collapse. Nevertheless, the indisputable fact remains that the invasion, set for November 1945, was unnecessary. Further, Japanese leaders attested that though beaten in the various Pacific island campaigns, there would have been no surrender but for the devastating bombing of the homeland.

Other critics of the strategic bomber attributed the Japanese surrender exclusively to the atomic bomb. Here too there is sufficient evidence to assert that economically and militarily Japan had already been defeated before the atomic bombs were used and that she would have been unable to sustain another three months of intense bombing at the rate planned – a tonnage equivalent to the total already delivered since B-29 operations began.

It is true that the sea blockade of Japan, to which the 20th AF contributed by minelaying, was a factor in defeat, owing to Japan's dependence on imported materials and food. Also the B-29 force could never have been in a position to strike but for the land-sea operations that secured the Marianas bases. Undeniably the interdependence of land, sea and air forces was essential in achieving victory in the Pacific but, speculative arguments apart, the evidence of the Japanese attests to the Superfortress raids as the principal cause of surrender.

Before the atomic weapons were used the bombing had depleted the economy to such an extent that key industries were nearing the point of complete disruption. Compared with war peaks, production at oil refineries was down to 17 per cent, aero-engine plants to 25 per cent, aircraft assembly to 40 per cent and electronic and allied equipment to 30 per cent, most of this stemming from small plants away from large industrial complexes. Vast quantities of other products and materials had been destroyed. Burned to the ground were 178 square miles of industrial areas which incapacitated production in sixty-one cities. A total of 602 principal war factories were identified as having been destroyed or severely crippled by bombs or resultant fires. The mines laid by B-29s had in the last few weeks of the war become the chief source of sinkings suffered by the Japanese mercantile marine – 80 per cent of this fleet was destroyed during hostilities and a 10 per cent share of the total was attributed to mines. Japanese records show that 300,000 people were killed, 433,000 injured and 9,200,000 made homeless by these raids – including the atomic bombs. The terrible destruction created by the bombers caused widespread disenchantment with the war and brought a mood of hopelessness to large sections of the population. The bombing was established as the most important factor in causing the Japanese people to feel certain of defeat and unwilling to continue the war.

5. Observations and Conclusions

At the end of World War II the USAAF's very heavy bomber and its atomic bombs dominated the military scene. The theory of strategic bombardment was valid through the sheer destructive power of the new weapon, sufficient numbers of which could decimate any nation in a matter of hours. In the light of this development few could deny that air power had a completely independent role. The autonomy the AAF leaders had persistently sought would no longer be denied them and a United States Air Force was created in 1947 from the semi-autonomous Army Air Forces. The strategic bomber, armed with nuclear weapons, would form the United States' principal deterrent force over the next decade and a half until land- and sea-launched missiles showed a better means of delivery.

The impact of the atomic weapon on military strategy did not blind General Arnold and his staff to lessons to be learned from the use of heavy bombers in both Europe and the Pacific wars. The findings of the Strategic Bombing Surveys, covering Germany and Japan, were well considered. A comparison of bombing campaigns conducted against the two nations is particularly interesting.

Germany was rightly recognised as the most dangerous enemy at an early date. Their production potential, technological standards and military expertise were probably without equal in 1939, ranking far above Japan's. Germany's resilience to aerial bombardment is shown by the fact that total tonnage of bombs dropped by the AAF alone was three times that directed against Japan. In Germany the people's will to resist was never a major factor in the nation's demise yet in Japan morale was failing many weeks before the end. In part this can be attributed to the concentration of destruction due to the fire-vulnerable areas in most Japanese cities, bringing far greater loss of life than in most individual raids on Germany.

Japan never mounted the formidable defences encountered over Hitler's Reich, evinced by the ratio of average heavy bomber losses to sorties – one loss to every sixty-seven sorties over Germany, and one to every 240 over Japan. The expenditure in terms of losses, casualties, sorties and ordnance was between three and four times greater against Germany yet this nation did not suffer really telling effect from strategic bombardment until the closing months of the war. Whereas strategic bombing succeeded overwhelmingly against Japan, the extent of its effect cannot be so precisely estimated in respect of·the European Axis, reflecting Germany's less vulnerable and more resilient economy.

Over Europe the strategic bombing effect had frequently been dissipated by diversion of the force available to secondary aims. As General Arnold later wrote: 'After a soundly conceived and carefully prepared strategic campaign has been launched, carry it through inexorably and without interruption. Diversion of effort to purposes of momentary importance will endanger the success of a whole air campaign.' This and other statements bear out the commanding general's apparent impatience with the rate of operations of both 8th and 20th AFs. Field commanders had been rather abruptly moved when Arnold felt a need to hasten action. If he appeared a hard task-master at the time – for it was more the situation rather than the command that deteriorated – his actions bore the mark of a determined leader

Originally a devotee of the doctrine of daylight precision bombardment, Arnold was quick to favour area attacks when they seemed a better means of hurrying the desired result. By the time Germany capitulated it was very evident that sporadic attacks on isolated industries, however accurate, were no substitute for persistent bombing in great volume of a range of vital associated industries. With the successful fire raids on Japanese cities Arnold and other AAF leaders came to accept the views of the early air strategists, that the population sustaining war production were as much a part of modern war as the military forces.

The strategic bomber had radically changed warfare. Horrific as its record might be in terms of death and destruction, there was a new awareness that never again would the military alone be subject to hostilities, for in total war the power of the new weapons would allow no discrimination between civilian and soldier; indeed in such a conflict decimation of an enemy's economy entailed massive destruction of centres of population. A new element of fear was born that no nation could afford to neglect.

The strategic bomber was not long exclusive to the United States and Britain in post-war years for the Russians, evidently impressed by the destruction found at targets in former German held territory, paid the compliment of putting into production an almost exact copy of the B-29 based on examples forced down in their territory during 1945.

The U.S. strategic bomber would appear again in the Korean war of 1950–1953 but largely in tactical roles for political reasons. Again, briefly, at the end of 1972, came a true strategic strike. Then with conventional bombs in great volume, aided by precise electronic guidance, the pattern evoked in Japan twenty-seven years before was repeated in North Vietnam with deadly effect. The potency still matched up to the visions of Trenchard and Mitchell.

6. The Arms

Aircraft

The basic instrument of strategic attack during World War II was the bomber aeroplane. With objectives a considerable distance from bases, range was of paramount importance and a sizeable bomb load the other prime factor. To accommodate the necessary fuel and bombs a large airframe was essential, necessitating ample power. In consequence air forces considering strategic bombing in the mid-1930s favoured multi-engined designs, the British accepting a 5 ton payload and 700 mile radius of action as sufficient to retaliate against their potential enemy, Nazi Germany. On the other hand Germany – and Japan – developed bombers of limited range for tactical purposes and neglected the strategic concept.

In the United States at this time, where strategic bombing was politically unacceptable, the heavy bomber was procured to strike at invading fleets, with the design emphasis on range, at the expense of bomb load. The B-17 Fortress, the first aircraft developed to meet this rather nebulous threat, had a 2 ton bomb load and 1,000 miles' radius of action. Both the later B-24 and B-29 designs had greater emphasis on range than ordnance, but the potential of the B-29 was such that it was eventually developed to haul a 10 ton bomb load over a 1,600 mile radius.

The use of these bombers in high altitude approach and attack methods pursued by the AAF, adversely affected bomb load and range. Operating from the U.K., AAF B-17s and B-24s had to gain a nominal 20,000 feet before crossing the enemy coastline to mitigate the accuracy of anti-aircraft artillery. This entailed orbiting over the U.K. for some two hours, during which time perhaps 350 to 400 miles of range were lost. Climbs to high altitude also caused high fuel consumption. These two factors restricted the combat radius to some 750 to 800 miles. A similar situation existed for heavy bombers operating from Italy but in Asian and Pacific theatres bombers could often climb to high altitude en route.

Other factors contributed to widely fluctuating performance capabilities of the bombers. For extreme range targets maximum fuel had to be carried and to keep to maximum safe take-off weight, bomb loads had to be restricted. At medium altitudes (10–15,000 feet) better fuel economy could often be obtained, giving increased range or alternatively reduced fuel and greater bomb load. In hostile airspace, such as over Germany, high altitude was a defensive necessity whereas, in the weeks immediately preceding Japan's surrender, B-29s were able to operate with near impunity at low to medium altitudes thus gaining considerably in performance and loads carried.

Heavy defensive armament was a feature of AAF heavy bombers, bestowed in the belief that with close formation tactics massing their guns they would survive against fighter attack on daylight missions. While these batteries of heavy machine guns did allow the bombers to force a passage, albeit at times hotly contested, the value of much of this armament was in doubt towards the end of hostilities. In Europe fighter escort became the principal means of deflecting enemy interceptors and bomber armament was being reduced (it was planned to remove nose and ball turrets from B-17s in the spring of 1945), while in the Pacific all but the tail defence of many B-29s was discarded and darkness used as a protective cloak.

Specifications and development details of the three strategic bombers follow. Prototypes and experimental versions are not included unless relevant.

BOEING B-17 FORTRESS

As described in Part 1 the B-17 was the aircraft around which the concept of high-altitude daylight bombardment was developed in the immediate pre-war period. The prototype was funded by Boeing for a design contest staged in 1935 resulting in orders for thirteen YB-17 models for service evaluation in 1936, delivered the following year. The YB-17A was the designation of a single experimental model used primarily to develop turbo-superchargers on the Wright 1820 radial engines during 1938–39. The B-17B followed in the winter of 1939–40 with turbo-superchargers for the engines and a redesigned nose section as major improvements for production of thirty-nine. These early B-17s, utilised for training when hostilities began, did not see combat.

Boeing B-17C and B-17D At the outbreak of war the AAF had fifty-eight Fortresses; forty-seven with first-line squadrons in the Philippines and Hawaii and most of the remainder with the 7th Bomb Group in the process of moving from the U.S.A. to the Philippines. Although the C and D models were the first Flying Fortresses with strategic bombardment capability, they were little used in such operations; those in war zones being all but eliminated.

Both B-17C and B-17D were built to the same contract (13257) awarded to Boeing, 20th September 1939 for thirty-eight model 299Hs with an option for additional machines. The B-17C, basically a more combat-worthy version of the B-17B, had improved defences, some crew armour and early leak-proof fuel tanks. Defensive armament was standardised on 0.50 calibre machine guns and all five gun positions were modified to give improved fields of fire and better facilities for the gunners. Only eighteen B-17Cs reached the Air Corps as twenty were sold to Britain. A contract change dated 17th April 1940 increased the B-17C order by another forty-two to a total of eighty but there were so many specified changes that this batch was given a new Army designation when put in production in the autumn of 1941. Outwardly, the B-17D could be distinguished from the C model by cooling flaps on the engine cowlings. Internally major changes involved a superior type of self-sealing tank better able to stand the rigours of combat and suitable for field repairs, a low-pressure oxygen system, revised armour plate, and 24 volt electrics in place of the 12 volt system. The dorsal and ventral gun positions each had twin 0.50 weapons on the D model in lieu of power-operated gun turrets awaited from production. Apart from cowl-ing flaps, most of these changes were also incorporated in the B-17Cs in the spring of 1941 so that there was little difference between the two models and both served together in operational squadrons. The B-17C and D were the fastest Flying Fortresses, having maximum speeds given as 323 mph by the Air Corps and 318 mph by Boeing at 25,000 feet. However, the RAF obtained 325 mph in their trials and in one lightly loaded flight to 35,000 feet British pilots claimed 350 mph true air speed. This capability, even for short periods, should have provided the B-17C and D with good escape potential from interceptors, but as both RAF and AAF discovered this was not the case. The defensive armament also proved inadequate, principally lack of guns to meet tail attacks and difficulty in delivering accurate fire with hand held weapons.

Only three groups used these model Fortresses operationally and all had been relegated to transport or training by the summer of 1942.

Specification of B-17C and D Power: Four Wright R-1820-65 Cyclone rated at a maximum 1,200 horse-power each for take-off. Wing span: 103 ft 9 in. Wing area: 1,420 sq ft. Fuselage length: 67 ft 10½ in. Empty weight: approximately 31,000 lb to full B-17D standard. General combat weight: approximately 40,000 lb including 2,000 lb bomb load. Maximum bomb load: 4,800 lb consisting of 8 × 600 lb bombs, alternatively 14 × 300 lb, 4 × 1,100 lb or 2 × 2,000 lb bombs. Normal internal fuel in six wing tanks was 1,700 U.S. gallons but a maximum of 2,492 could be accommodated on long range ferry flights when two 396 gallon capacity tanks were installed in the bomb bay. On long range combat flights one of these bomb bay tanks was often retained, but this halved the bomb load. Maximum range with 4,000 lb bombs at 25,000 ft at 225 mph was in the region of 2,000 miles varying through atmospheric conditions and pilotage. Initial rate of climb was approximately 1,200 ft per minute and it took 7.5 minutes to reach 10,000 feet. Operational altitude of 20,000 feet could be reached in 20 minutes and the service ceiling was 37,800 feet. Armament consisted of 6 × 0.50-in calibre Brownings and one 0.30-in machine gun; all hand-manipulated. A single 0.50 gun was situated at each of the fuselage waist hatches. Twin 0.50s were placed in the upper fuselage emplacement and in the ventral compartment, both with rearward fields of fire. The single 0.30 gun was fired through any one of four sockets in the nosepiece. A total of 3,000 rounds of 0.50 ammunition was authorised and five hundred of the smaller calibre for the nose gun. A crew of seven was standard: pilot and co-pilot; navigator and bombardier in the nose compartment; three gunners, the dorsal gunner combining duties with radio operator. An eighth member, aircraft commander, was often carried in a lead bomber seated just behind the pilot.

Boeing B-17E The first B-17 aircraft specifically intended for offensive strategic operations, the B-17E incorporated major design changes improving stability for bombing from very high altitudes and introducing defensive armament worthy of the name Fortress. Work on this version was started before the B-17C's shortcomings were revealed by the RAF. The initial contract for 512 B-17Es (Boeing 299 0), went to Boeing 30th August 1940. Trials of high-altitude precision bombing with the B-17B had indicated some instability when the flight control mechanism on the Norden bombsight was locked in for a bombing run. This took the form of yawing, sometimes quite viciously. To prevent this a larger tail was designed, double the previous area. Power operated turrets, then a feature of modern British bombers, were under development by some three companies in the U.S.A., an upper turret and a remotely controlled under turret being developed by Bendix specifically for the B-17.

A vital requirement was for a tail gun position to meet fighter attack from astern. To include such an installation it was necessary to redesign the fuselage from a station just aft of the wing root, giving it an even taper terminating in a raised cockpit for the gunner with a housing for two 0.50 guns. The gunner's hood was faired into the base of the fin. The manually controlled guns were linked to a simple bead sight in front of the gunner's window, through a bell crank mechanism. While the arrangement did not give the stability or field of fire afforded by most power operated turrets, it was considerably lighter and quite effective in conjunction with the other armament covering the rear. The Sperry upper power turret was very compact and had a lower profile than British turrets, providing less drag but not allowing the guns to depress below the horizontal. The lower turret used periscope sighting and although put into production was found impractical by gunners who were given the near impossible task of tracking enemy fighters with it. In any case Sperry had a manned ventral turret under development and this was installed on the 113th and subsequent B-17Es. Popularly known as the 'ball turret' this had an excellent all-round field of fire below the horizontal plane and was extremely compact. The two guns were fixed and revolved with the turret, which was set on a heavy brass gear suspended by a tripod structure within the bomber's fuselage. The gunner, entering the 'ball' from the fuselage, sat in a hunched but comfortable position between the two guns backing the armour-plated door. It was, however, not a position for a large man and ball gunners were usually of small stature. The two waist window positions were retained in the B-17E but were now of rectangular shape. The forward portion of the aircraft was basically as the B-17D with no changes in nose defences. A total of 1,023 B-17Es were built.

Empty, the B-17E was some 1,500 lb heavier than the D model and performance suffered by the extra drag of the larger tail surfaces and the turrets, but only marginally.

The first B-17Es were being despatched to the Pacific when the Japanese struck Pearl Harbour and during the first six months of the war nearly 100 B-17Es were sent to aid defences in the Pacific area. Used by the 7th BG in the battle for Java, and then as replacements for the 19th BG flying from Australia against targets in New Guinea, the residue were turned over to the 43rd BG when it relieved the 19th in the autumn of 1942. The 5th and 11th Groups in Hawaii were both re-equipped with B-17Es early in 1942 and subsequently moved to the 13th Air Force in the New Hebrides for the assault on Guadalcanal. These two groups were largely employed in ocean patrol until the Fortresses were withdrawn from Pacific service during 1943. While not involved in any planned strategic campaign, a few operations had strategic intent.

Some fifty B-17Es were sent to Europe, most with the 97th Bomb Group, first of the heavy bomber units assigned to the 8th Air Force. They flew the eight opening missions of the Force's campaign before transfer to the 92nd Bomb Group, then primarily charged with operation training. A few

B-17Es were used operationally in the Middle East during the same year. Rendered obsolete by the F model, most B-17Es were employed in training organisations in the United States after 1942.

Specification B-17E Power, wing span, and area as B-17D. Fuselage length: 73 ft 10 in. Empty weight: approximately 32,250 lb. General combat weight: approximately 51,000 lb including 4,000 lb bomb load. Maximum bomb load: 4,000 lb consisting of 8 × 500 lb bombs, or 16 × 250 lb, or 4 × 1,000 lb or 2 × 2,000 lb. Normal internal fuel in wing tanks, 1,730 U.S. gallons. A maximum of 2,520 gallons could be carried on ferry flights using two bomb bay tanks of 396 U.S. gallons capacity. On combat flights one of these tanks could be retained in lieu of half bomb load to obtain extended range. Maximum range at optimum operating altitude of 25,000 ft was 2,000 miles at normal combat cruise speed of 180 mph, but variable depending on operational factors. Maximum speed was approximately 317 mph at 25,000 ft. Initial rate of climb was approximately 1,100 ft per minute and it took 7.1 minutes to reach 10,000 ft and 25 to attain 20,000 ft. Service ceiling was 36,500 ft with light loadings. Armament consisted of 8 × 0.50-in calibre machine guns and a single 0.30-in weapon. A single 0.50 was located in each waist position hatch, twin 0.50s in the tail emplacement and each of the two power turrets. The single 0.30 defended the nose. A total of 3,600 rounds of 0.50 ammunition was detailed plus 500 rounds of 0.30 calibre. In Pacific war zones head-on attacks by Japanese fighters brought numerous local modifications to increase the nose armament, often dispensing with the 0.30 weapon completely. The most popular mount was two, sometimes one, hand-held 0.50s through an aperture cut in the upper part of the nose-piece, but variations included up to four guns in the nose. B-17Es reaching Europe had two 'cheek' guns mounted through the side windows of the nose for use by the navigator. Crew ten. Four officers, six enlisted men. Pilot and co-pilot left and right of cockpit respectively. Navigator positioned in nose compartment with bombardier, both acting as gunners. Engineer doubling as top turret gunner. Radio-operator in compartment aft of bomb bay. Two waist, a ball turret and a rear gunner.

Boeing B-17F First ordered on a Defence Aid contract dated 2nd June 1941, the B-17F made use of a Cyclone engine with improved high-altitude output and wide-blade propellers giving better performance in tropical conditions. Carburettor intake filters were fitted to prolong engine life in dusty conditions. This Fortress embodied many revisions and additions to the basic model E, although the only notable external change was a frameless nose transparency. (Boeing model designation was still 299 0.) With higher loadings, the undercarriage was strengthened and a dual brake system fitted. Revision of bomb-bay stowage allowed bombs for a greater payload to be carried. Most notable armament change was an improved ball turret, also the oxygen system efficiency and reliability was improved.

B-17Fs destined for combat theatres passed through modification centres where the most notable addition was the installation of large nose side windows through which additional 0.50 calibre guns were installed.

Initial production was from Boeing, Seattle, but new Lockheed Vega and Douglas plants in California were in production with B-17Fs by the fall of 1942. It took some months for these factories to get into their stride but by the spring of 1943 some twelve B-17Fs a day were being produced. They were reaching the AAF from June 1942; the first group fully equipped, the 92nd BG, moved to the U.K. in August 1942. By summer 1943 the 8th AF in England had sixteen bomb groups equipped with this model and the 12th AF had four groups operating from North Africa. Apart from approximately fifty B-17Fs sent to the SWPA as replacements, August-September 1942, the bulk of production went to combat groups in Europe and North Africa.

A total of 3,405 B-17Fs were produced by the three factories between May 1942 and September 1943, during which time numerous detail changes were made involving twenty-nine production block numbers (indicating changes not warranting a model designation change). The most significant was the inclusion of so-called Tokyo tanks from Boeing block 80, Douglas 25 and Vega 30. These tanks, five cells in each outer main-plane section, had a total capacity of 1,080 U.S. gallons, bolstering the maximum capacity of the B-17F to 2,810 gallons and substantially improving endurance. On later B-17Fs provision was also made for an external rack under each wing enabling the bomb load to be doubled, although at a considerable range penalty.

After the 8th AF had experimented with various local modifications to improve defence a dozen experimental gunships were produced by Vega armed with fourteen 0.50 guns, including two in a second upper turret, and two in a remotely controlled under-nose turret – that came to be known as the 'chin turret'. Designated YB-40s a few other examples reached the 8th AF but, like the original batch, were found to have no protective advantage to the formations with which they flew.

Surviving B-17Fs were withdrawn from combat squadrons in England and Italy in the autumn of 1944 primarily due to the superior engine accessory systems, notably electric in place of hydraulic control of turbo-superchargers, of the succeeding B-17G.

Specification B-17F Power: Four Wright R-1820-97 Cyclone radials rated at a maximum 1,200 hp each for take off. Wing span and area as B-17E. Fuselage length: 74 ft 9 in. Empty weight: approximately 34,000 lb. General combat weight: approximately 56,500 lb with 6,000 lb bombs. Normal bomb load on long-range missions was 4,000 lb. A B-17F had the capability on very short haul missions of lifting a 20,800 lb bomb load using external racks for 2 × 4,000 lb bombs plus 8 × 1,600 lb bombs in the bay. In practice maximum loads were usually in the region of 6,000 lb. The bomb bay could accommodate 26 × 100 lb, or 16 × 300 lb, or 12 × 500 lb or 6 × 1,000 lb or 2 × 2,000 lb types. External racks were generally used for 1,000 lb or 2,000 lb. Internal fuel tankage was 1,730 U.S. gallons in early models but additional tanks in the outer wing sections of B-17F-80-BO, B-17F-25-DL, and B-17F-30-VE models gave an extra 1,080 U.S. gallons. With bomb bay tanks, capacity could be as high as 3,630 U.S. gallons for ferry flights. Maximum range of optimum combat altitude of 25,000 ft was some 2,000 miles, but effective maximum combat range was about 1,700 miles giving a radius of action of 850 miles. It took 25.7 minutes to reach 20,000 ft at 55,000 lb gross weight and the service ceiling was 37,500 ft. Maximum speed approximately 300 mph at 25,000 ft. Normal combat cruise speed 165–180 mph. Armament was originally as specified for the B-17E, but the 0.30

alibre weapon was soon deleted and by early 1943 B-17Fs were being despatched overseas with 11 × 0.50 Brownings and provision for a total 4,430 rounds of ammunition. These guns were located, two each in the tail position and upper and lower turrets, one in each waist window, the radio room upper hatch, and in the 'cheek' windows either side of the nose. In the U.K. an additional one or two 0.50s were placed in the nose firing through an aperture cut in the glazing. These had limited flexibility and restricted the bombardier's space so were not usually fitted in lead bombers. Eventually depots undertaking this work standardised on a single weapon. Crew ten. Pilot and co-pilot, navigator and bombardier in nose compartment. Flight engineer doubling as top turret gunner, radio-operator/gunner in radio room aft of bomb bay. Two waist gunners and a ball turret and tail gunner.

BOEING B-17G

The B-17G replaced the B-17F in production during the late summer of 1943. The ultimate combat configuration of the Fortress, and by far the largest production for any model, 8,680 were produced by Boeing, Douglas and Lockheed-Vega plants, with production terminating in April, June and July of 1945 respectively.

The B-17G was distinguished from the B-17F by its 'chin' turret, first tried out on the experimental YB-40 escort version of the Fortress. The installation was made to the last batch of Douglas built B-17Fs but these were redesignated as Gs. This twin gun turret, operated remotely by the bombardier, obviated the installation of hand-manipulated guns in the frontal transparency and allowed greater freedom of movement in the nose. The B-17G also incorporated minor changes to the navigator's facilities and the resiting of equipment displaced by the chin turret installation. With the Boeing and Douglas plant blocks 35 and Vega block 25, the General Electric B-22 high-speed supercharger was installed on the engines giving better high-altitude performance when heavily loaded, raising the combat ceiling. Armament changes featured the staggering of the two fuselage waist positions and fitting enclosing gun windows to give better conditions for the gunners. These changes were introduced on the Boeing and Vega blocks 50 and Douglas block 35, and many older B-17s in service were modified to this standard. An improved tail gun position, giving a greater field of fire, better gunner comfort and a new sight, was introduced with the Boeing block 80, Douglas block 45 and Vega block 55. It was commonly known as the 'Cheyenne' tail turret from its origins at the Wyoming modification centre of that name. On later production B-17Gs the radio operator's gun mount was embodied in an enclosed window after the fashion of the waist guns, but towards the end of production the gun was deleted altogether; both the 8th and 15th Air Forces had ceased to consider this defence point of practical value. These air forces also dispensed with one waist gunner late in 1944 when enemy air activity declined. There were also crew armour changes and, towards the end of production, flak curtains began to supercede armour plate in some positions.

B-17Gs began to arrive in Europe as replacements in September 1943, the first group to be despatched with this model as original equipment, the 401st BG, arrived in England in November that year. Subsequently four more groups were despatched to the 8th AF and two to the 15th AF, while

B-17G: Crew stations and defensive fire-power.

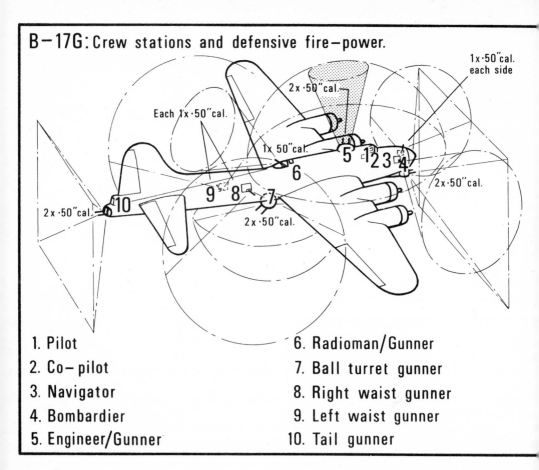

1x·50"cal. each side

2x·50"cal.

Each 1x·50"cal.

1x 50"cal.

2x·50"cal.

2x·50"cal.

2x·50"cal.

1. Pilot
2. Co-pilot
3. Navigator
4. Bombardier
5. Engineer/Gunner

6. Radioman/Gunner
7. Ball turret gunner
8. Right waist gunner
9. Left waist gunner
10. Tail gunner

five B-24 groups in the 8th AF converted to B-17Gs July – October 1944. The twenty groups already in action in Europe had largely re-equipped with B-17Gs by the previous spring.

Specification B-17G Power, wing span and area as B-17F. Fuselage length: 74 ft 9 in on early aircraft, 74 ft 4 in with Cheyenne tail turret. Empty weight: approximately 36,135 lb. General combat weight: approximately 65,500 lb with 6,000 lb bombs. Normal bomb load on long range missions was 4,000 lb. An extreme maximum load of 20,800 lb could be carried making use of external racks but in practice maximum loads to short-haul targets were in the region of 6,000 lb. The bomb bay accommodated 8 × 1,600 lb bombs maximum load. More usual loads were 12 × 500 lb or 6 × 1,000 lb or 4 × 1,600 lb, or 2 × 2,000 lb GP. Internal fuel capacity allowed a maximum 2,810 gallons, giving about 2,000 miles range at 180 mph with a gross take-off weight of 65,500 lb. The maximum effective range was, as late B-17Fs, in the region of 1,700 miles, making a radius of action of 850 miles. It took 37 minutes to reach 20,000 feet with a take-off weight of 65,500 lb under ideal conditions. Service ceiling was 35,600 feet. Maximum speed was approximately 287 mph at 25,000 ft but operational cruise speed was, as the B-17F, in the 165–185 mph bracket. Armament

omprised thirteen guns of 0.50-in calibre; two each in the chin, upper, ball
nd tail turrets, one each in the nose cheek positions and waist windows. Also
single gun in the radio compartment, deleted during the latter part of 1944
y combat units and later from production aircraft. Crew ten; later nine.
ilot and co-pilot; navigator and bombardier in nose compartment;
ngineer also acting as upper turret gunner; radio operator in compartment
ft of bomb-bay. Two waist gunners (later only one), ball turret and tail
unner.

ONSOLIDATED B-24 LIBERATOR

The prototype (Convair Type 32) was ordered in late March 1939 to
eet requirements for a heavy bomber with an all-round performance
uperior to that of the B-17. Consolidated's experience had been chiefly
 design and construction of large flying boats; the XB-24 was com-
leted and flown in nine months through utilising the Davis wing and
rge twin fins and rudders already tested on an experimental flying boat.
he Davis wing airfoil, of particularly good aerodynamic characteristics,
ave the B-24 series its distinctive narrow tapering wing of high aspect ratio.
roduction aircraft began leaving the San Diego plant late 1940 and most
f these early bombers were delivered to British orders. Design development
p to American involvement in World War II resulted in a reworked proto-
ype, a test version and two models in production, totalling 192 aircraft of
hich around a third went to Britain. Refinement were embodied in the
rst major model, the B-24D, produced from early November 1941 to
eptember 1943 with little change in form. With superior range, payload
nd performance to the B-17, the B-24 was earmarked for greater quantity
roduction and ultimately five plants assembled these bombers. More
iberators were built than any other U.S. military aircraft in World War II.
part from armament no fundamental changes were made in the design of
arge-scale production models, with the exception of the nose turret.

Consolidated B-24D The first combat-worthy Liberator for the AAF; in
roduction at San Diego for twenty months on eight different contracts
early examples were on YB-24 and B-24A contracts) totalling 2,425,
nvolving thirty-five different production blocks. With Government aid
onsolidated opened a second plant at Forth Worth, Texas, in 1942 where
03 D models were subsequently built, Douglas operated a plant in Tulsa,
klahoma, soon afterwards and built ten B-24Ds. The overall plan for
iberator production involved the Ford Motor Company, brought in to
pply its expertise with mass production techniques to B-24 sub-assemblies
hich were supplied to Consolidated Fort Worth and Douglas, Tulsa, but
ord also started their own assembly line. Identical to B-24Ds, all Liberators
ssembled from Ford sub-assemblies by the three plants were given the
esignation B-24E to identify their origin. The fifth B-24 manufacturer,
orth American at Dallas, Texas, had their version designated B-24G.
he majority of B-24E and early B-24G models were used for training in the
.S.A. and few examples saw service in the war zones.

The first San Diego built B-24Ds were delivered with two 0.50-in calibre
uns in both rear and upper powered turrets and a single 0.50 for firing
hrough socket points in the nose. No defence was provided for the under-
ides. With block 25 from San Diego, the nose armament was bolstered by a

further two hand-manipulated 0.50s and another gun was installed in eac
fuselage waist window giving the B-24D a total of ten 0.50s. Then a retrac
able periscope sighted turret was added for under defence, but foun
impracticable: less than 300 B-24Ds had this item. Following aircraft ha
provision for a single 0.50 weapon firing through the hatch in the rear fuse
age floor, although the field of fire was severely restricted. In the 140 bloc
and all subsequent production from San Diego, the Briggs/Sperry ba
turret was installed. Unlike the ball turret on the B-17, that on the B-24 wa
retractable because of limited ground clearance. Numerous field modifica
tions were carried out to improve armament: the 8th AF fitted a paired mou
of 0.50s firing through a large aperture cut in the nose in similar fashion to th
improvised installation on B-17Fs. B-24Ds operating in the Pacific wei
modified at the Hawaiian depot to take a tail turret in the nose, providin
superior frontal defence to meet Japanese fighter attacks predominantl
made from this quarter.

The four self-sealing fuel tanks in the wing centre section held 2,364 U.S
gallons but with block 1 from San Diego an additional tank was placed i
each outer wing section raising the total to 2,814. Wide-blade propelle
came into use with block 15 to give better operation in tropical condition

Specification B-24D Power: Four Pratt-Whitney R-1830-43 Twin Was
radials (later production had R-1830-65 engines featuring different make (
carburettor) rated at 1,200 horse-power each for take-off. Wing span: 110 f
Wing area: 1,048 sq ft. Fuselage length: 66 ft 4 in. Empty weight: 34,000 ll
General combat loaded weight approximately 63,500 lb with 5,000 lb bomb
for late models while early B-24Ds grossed some 3,000 lb less with an equiva
lent payload. Normal bomb load for a long-range mission was about 5,000 lt
An 8,000 lb load could be accommodated on short-range missions an
maximum internal load was 12,800 lb when 8 × 1,600 lb armour-piercin
bombs were carried. Alternative loads could be: 20 × 100 lb, or 12 × 300 ll
or 8 × 1,000 lb, or 4 × 2,000 lb. Because of the high gross weight and fu
requirements heavy loads would not be carried on the strategic operation
flown in Europe. Internal fuel tankage was 2,814 U.S. gallons, in all but th
very early Ds, and with two 400 U.S. gallon bomb bay tanks the capacit
for ferry flights could be 3,164. Extreme range at 25,000 ft was 2,300 mile
at maximum cruise speed of 215 mph but combat range over Europe wa
some 1,700 miles at 20,000 ft at 190 mph, giving a radius of action of 85
miles. At 56,000 lb gross it took 22 minutes to reach 20,000 ft. Service ceilin
was 28,000 ft. Maximum speed was 303 mph at 25,000 ft. Armament on th
late battle-proofed B-24Ds consisted of three flexible 0.50s in the nose, tw
each in the tail, ball and upper turrets and one in each waist window makin
a total of ten. Total ammunition provision was 3,800 rounds. Crew ter
Pilot and co-pilot, bombardier and navigator in nose, radio operator a
pilot's cabin, engineer also acting as top turret gunner, two waist gunner
ball gunner and tail gunner.

Consolidated B-24H The need for a power-operated turret to comb
head-on attacks by enemy fighters was met by a new factory model in Jun
1943. An electrically operated turret designed by the Emerson compan
proved more responsive and was thought less vulnerable than the hydrauli
Consolidated model used in the tail. The B-24H designation was given t

ord-built aircraft with nose turrets and also to those of Forth Worth and
'ulsa which used Ford sub-assemblies. Of a total 3,100 H models, Ford
·roduced 1,780 in ten months, Fort Worth 738 in nine months and Douglas
'ulsa 582 in eight months. North American, Dallas commenced production
·f an equivalent model at the end of 1943 but these still carried the designa-
ion B-24G, the same as that of the first 25 D configuration Liberators from
his plant. The nose-turret versions commenced with block 1 production
hange and a total of 406 B-24Gs were built in six months. In all other
espects the initial B-24H and B-24G-1-NT aircraft were as the B-24E and
arly G models they replaced.

The new turret was heavy bringing the total empty weight of the B-24H
o 36,500 lb, and causing drag it reduced top speed by some 13 mph. The
;ross weight advanced to 65,000 lb, but was often exceeded in war theatres
vhere it was not uncommon for the take-off weight of a B-24H to be in
·xcess of 72,000 lb. With such overloads flying could be hazardous in bad
veather. Never an easy aircraft to fly at high altitude or in formation, a heavily
oaded B-24 called for constant physical effort at the controls. The most
dverse effect of the nose turret was its restriction of the bombardier's
:ompartment limiting his vision during target runs.

Major improvements made to the B-24H series during production in-
:luded the new high-speed GE B-22 model turbo-supercharger in the 15th
)lock onwards at all four sources of manufacture. This gave improved
)erformance at altitude but this was balanced out in war theatres by even
iigher loadings. In later production, waist gun hatches were glazed over to
)rotect gunners from the elements.

First B-24H unit was the 392nd BG sent to the 8th AF in August 1943.
[hree other groups arriving in the U.K. late 1943 also had B-24Hs and a
'urther fourteen groups following in the first four months of 1944 were also
argely equipped with this model. Thirteen groups joining the 15th AF in
taly during the same period also had a preponderance of B-24Hs but three
;roups had a number of B-24Gs as original equipment. North American
)roduction of late B-24G appears to have gone almost exclusively to the
l5th Air Force. Many B-24Hs endured in first-line squadrons until the end of
he war.

Consolidated B-24J This designation applied to a model intended to bring
;ome standardisation to all five sources of Liberator production. Initially,
iowever, the B-24J designation applied solely to the home plant at San
Diego when a nose turret was first installed, beginning August 1943. This
urret was originally a Consolidated design, similar to the standard tail
urret, but with block 210 the Emerson turret was used. The San Diego J
nodel introduced a new automatic pilot and an improved bombsight,
'eatures that when incorporated on production in the other four plants
)rought the J designation. The termination of the H and G models and their
·eplacement by the J commenced at Willow Run in April 1944, and at Tulsa,
Fort Worth and Dallas in May 1944. Because Liberator production was more
:han meeting requirements of the U.S. services and America's allies, the
B-24J was terminated at Forth Worth (after 1,558 in December 1944), Tulsa
(in July 1944 with the 205th J) and North American (after 536 in November
1944). These plants went over to other military types.

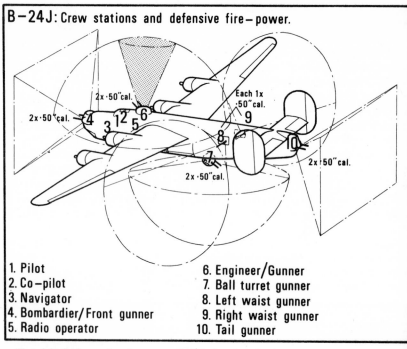

B−24J: Crew stations and defensive fire−power.

1. Pilot
2. Co−pilot
3. Navigator
4. Bombardier/Front gunner
5. Radio operator
6. Engineer/Gunner
7. Ball turret gunner
8. Left waist gunner
9. Right waist gunner
10. Tail gunner

Total B-24J production was 6,678, by far the largest production of an
Liberator model. Production changes were generally of a minor nature an
there was some variance in the turret models installed. In combat zone
B-24Js were received chiefly as replacements although two groups to the 8t
AF and one to the Pacific had been sent out in the spring of 1944 with
San Diego aircraft original equipment. Like the B-24H, the J model had it
ball turret removed for operations with the 8th AF after midsummer 1944
Specification was very similar to that of the B-24H.

Consolidated B-24L This designation was originally introduced to mark a
system where theatre-specified tail armament would be installed at modifica
tion centres. The project was abandoned and the B-24Ls from Consolidate
and Ford were generally fitted with a tail-gun position featuring han
manipulated weapons – much after the successful installation in late B-17Gs
The purpose was to reduce weight but the 500 lb saved had no practical effec
on performance but did improve pilotage qualities. Otherwise the 1,66
B-24Ls built differed little from the late production B-24Js it succeeded.

Consolidated B-24M This model was supposed to standardise on a light
weight turret but as with the B-24L other types of tail-gun position were ofte
installed. Extra scanning windows were fitted in the nose to improve th
bombardier's outlook and on the 20th block from Ford the cockpit cabi
glazing was revised to improve visibility. This model was basically as th
B-24J with little difference in performance. A total of 916 B-24Ms wer
delivered by Consolidated and 1,677 by Ford.

Specification B-24G (from block 1), B-24H, B-24J, B-24L and B-24M
Power: Four Pratt-Whitney R-1830-65 Twin Wasp radials rated at 1,20

orse-power each for take-off. Wing span and area as B-24D. Fuselage length: 67 ft 2 in (B-24J 67 ft 7 in).* Empty weight: approximately 36,500 lb. General combat weight: 65,000 lb with 5,000 lb bombs. Normal bomb load for long-range missions in Europe 4,000 lb. A maximum bomb load of 12,800 lb could be accommodated internally if 1,600 lb armour-piercing bombs were used, but such a weight could only be carried on short-range missions. Alternative loads could be 20 × 100 lb, or 12 × 500 lb, or 8 × 1,000 lb or 4 × 2,000 lb. Fuel provision was 2,814 U.S. gallons with a maximum load of 3,614 if bomb-bay tanks used. Maximum range at 25,000 ft was 2,100 miles at 215 mph. Effective combat range was some 1,700 miles at 185 mph cruise at 21,000 ft on European missions, giving a radius of action of 800 miles. At 56,000 lb gross it took 25 minutes to reach 20,000 ft. Service ceiling was 28,000 ft. Maximum speed was 290 mph at 25,000 ft. Standard armament consisted of nose, tail, ball and upper turrets with two 0.50 calibre guns each and another of these weapons mounted in each waist window. A total of 4,700 rounds of ammunition was provided, with an increase to 5,200 rounds on later blocks to cater for the waist guns. In combat zones armament changes involved the removal of the ball turret by 8th AF to save weight from mid-1944. Removal of front turret in lead aircraft of 15th AF to provide more room for bombardier, and deletion of waist guns in the Pacific. Crew ten, later nine. Pilot and co-pilot; bombardier and navigator in nose, former acting as gunner (in lead aircraft a waist gunner moved to the nose turret while the bombardier was at his sight); engineer/top turret gunner, radio operator, two waist gunners (reduced to one in both 8th and 15th AF during last six months of war and eliminated altogether in many Pacific units); ball gunner (eliminated in 8th AF from mid-1944) and tail gunner.

BOEING B-29 SUPERFORTRESS

The only very heavy bomber used operationally by the AAF during World War II, the Superfortress stemmed from an Air Corps requirement of January 1940 for an aircraft with a 5,000 mile range and 2,000 lb bomb load to meet the needs of the United States' 'hemisphere defence' stance.

Four companies, Boeing, Lockheed, Douglas and Consolidated, submitted proposals, those of Boeing and Consolidated – designated XB-29 and XB-32 respectively – being awarded contracts for prototypes. The Boeing was considered the major project while the XB-32 was developed as a back-up type in the event of some unforeseen and insurmountable difficulty with the XB-29. Both companies' prototypes made their first flights in the late summer of 1942, the Boeing being particularly impressive and handling well for such a large aircraft. Thereafter the B-32 development lagged and only a few service versions saw combat towards the end of hostilities with Japan, but not in a strategic bombing role.

The XB-29 was not without problems, notably with the Wright R-3350 engines, new 2,200 horse-power-rated radials troubled by fires and failures. Engine fires precipitated the crash of the second XB-29 in February 1943. Three prototypes were followed by fourteen YB-29 test examples coming from Boeing's Wichita, Kansas, factory; the Company's main plant at Seattle being fully absorbed with B-17 assembly. In addition to Wichita, Boeing

* Fuselage length varied with different nose- and tail-turret combinations.

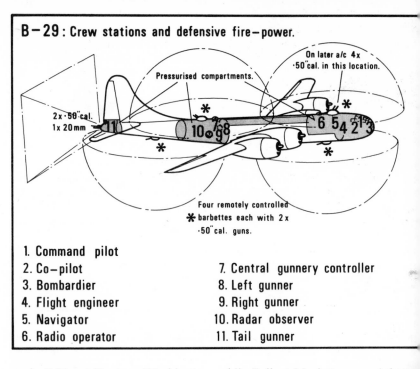

B-29 : Crew stations and defensive fire-power.

Pressurised compartments.

On later a/c 4x
·50˝cal. in this location.

2x·50˝cal.
1x 20mm

Four remotely controlled
✷ barbettes each with 2x
·50˝cal. guns.

1. Command pilot
2. Co-pilot
3. Bombardier
4. Flight engineer
5. Navigator
6. Radio operator
7. Central gunnery controller
8. Left gunner
9. Right gunner
10. Radar observer
11. Tail gunner

made B-29s at Renton, Washington, while Bell at Marietta near Atlanta, Georgia, and Martin at Omaha, Nebraska, also assembled the bombers. All told 3,960 B-29s had been produced at the four plants when production was terminated at Renton in May 1946.

Novel features of the B-29 were three pressurised crew compartments which maintained an 8,000-ft cabin pressure from that height up to 30,000 ft. The forward compartment, housing six crew members, was linked by a tube passage to a section aft of the bomb bays for three gunners and a radar operator. The tail gunner's compartment was the third pressurised section but the gunner could not move to another pressurised section at high altitude.

The B-29 was the first AAF aircraft to incorporate a fire-control system for remotely controlled armament. Four gun turrets, strategically located along the fuselage, were operated by gunners using computing sights in adjacent scanning domes. Control of a turret could shift from one gunner to another as a target aircraft passed from view of a particular scanning dome. The tail turret was part of this system and could be fired by a side blister gunner as far as his sight allowed. Tail armament consisted of two 0.50-in guns and a 20-mm cannon, but because of its slower rate of fire and different trajectory to the 0.50s the cannon was later deleted.

The speedy development of such an advanced and complex bomber as the B-29 brought numerous technical problems, particularly when the aircraft were first committed to gross combat loadings. The Wright engines gave serious trouble through inadequate cooling and lubrication of the exhaust valves on the upper rear cylinders, Baffles to provide better cooling and piping to conduct more oil to the troubled area were incorporated in early modifications. The high ground temperatures at Asiatic bases, sometimes 120 degrees F, were often in excess of the maximum specified carburettor air temperatures. Overheating brought reduction in power estimated at 200 horse-power in extreme cases. Limitation of taxiing time, take-off at dawn and dusk, were measures taken to restrict engine temperatures. Overheating in flight sometimes occurred through improper power/cowl flap relation, later circumvented by the introduction of shortened cowl flaps to cause less drag.

Propeller pitch mechanisms were modified to obtain additional rpm and lessen partial failure through oil congealing at high altitude. Other modifications were effected to prevent jamming of the pitch governor. Average engine change period was 150 hours by the spring of 1945 instead of 400 hours as designed. Later models of the R-3350 were more durable.

Other changes made to the B-29 included better aerodynamically balanced rudders, improved warm air heating of transparent panels to prevent frosting at altitude, deletion of electric crew stove and de-icing equipment on late production examples. Bomb bay doors were changed from electric to pneumatic operation to provide faster operation. Strengthened scanning dome transparencies and gunner securing harness were incorporated after incidents where pressurisation strain had caused the domes to burst and gunners to be sucked out of the aircraft.

The long range of the B-29 was utilised in photographic reconnaissance flights by both XX BC and XXI BC. In the autumn of 1944 a number of Superfortresses were equipped with various camera installations and suitably modified for this task under the designation F-13A. A squadron of F-13As operated as part of the 20th AF from November 1944 until the end of hostilities.

Boeing B-29 All 1,620 B-29-BWs built by Boeing Wichita between September 1943 and October 1945 used the basic B-29 designation with production block numbers indicating changes. This also applied to 357 B-29-BA made by Bell Atlanta between February 1944 and January 1945, and 536 assembled by Martin Omaha between January 1944 and September 1945, although this latter plant did not get into quantity production until midsummer 1944.

The first major change was an increase in fuel capacity by installing four extra fuel tanks in the wing centre section. These had a total capacity of 1,270 U.S. gallons raising the overall fuel load from a maximum 8,168 to 9,438 U.S. gallons. The change was made with the B-29-25-BW block from Wichita and the B-29-5-BA block from Bell while all Martin-built Superfortresses incorporated the new tanks apart from the first few pre-production aircraft. The four-gun upper turret, and strengthened sighting domes were first introduced on blocks B-29-40-BW, while Bell brought in the turret on B-29-10-BA and the new domes on the B-29-20-BA. All but pre-production Martin B-29s had the four-gun turret and the dome change was made with B-29-20-MO. The B-29-50-BW block introduced R-3350-41 engines with baffles and oil cross-over pipes to improve cooling and both Martin and Bell brought them in on block 20. The 20-mm tail cannon was eliminated with the B-29-55-BW, B-29-25-BA and B-29-25-MO. Later production from all plants had R-3350-57 engines.

Specification of B-29 Power: Four Wright R-3350-23 Cyclone radials rated at 2,200 horse-power each for take-off. Later production had -41 and

-57 improved models. Wing span: 141 ft 3 in. Wing area: 1,736 sq ft. Fuselage length: 99 ft. Empty weight: 70,140 lb for original production versions. General war loaded weight: 135,000 lb with 12,000 lb bombs. Normal bomb load for a 1,600-mile radius mission was 5,000 lb at high altitude. With weight reductions at medium altitude 12,000 lb was possible over the same distance. Maximum bomb load was 20,000 lb. The bomb bay could accommodate 4 × 4,000 lb or 8 × 2,000 lb or 12 × 1,600 lb or 12 × 1,000 lb or 40 × 500 lb. Internal fuel tankage was 8,198 U.S. gallons on early models and 9,548 U.S. gallons maximum on later models. Removal of semi-permanent bomb bay tanks could reduce the fuel to 6,988 U.S. gallons. Maximum range at optimum combat altitude of 25,000 ft was 3,250 miles with full fuel and 5,000 lb bombs for aircraft prior to B-29-25-BW and B-29-5-BA. Later models had 4,100-mile range under these conditions. Maximum ferry ranges for early and late models were 5,600 and 6,000 miles respectively while practical radius of action was 1,600 miles and 1,800 respectively. Time to 20,000 ft at 110,000 lb gross was 38 minutes and service ceiling was 31,850 ft. Maximum speed 357 mph at 25,000 ft. Normal combat cruise speed 200–220 mph. Armament comprised ten 0.50-in calibre guns and one 20-mm cannon in early aircraft. The cannon and two 0.50s were located in the tail turret and the other 0.50s each in four remote-controlled power turrets, part of a General Electric fire-control system. A four-0.50 gun turret was fitted commencing B-29-40-BW and B-29-10-BA blocks and cannon deleted with B-29-55-BW, B-29-25-BA and B-29-25-MO. Crew eleven, but varied in service. Command pilot and co-pilot; bombardier, navigator, flight engineer, radio operator in forward pressure cabin; central fire control gunner (rear upper blister); two side gunners and radar operator in mid-fuselage pressure cabin; and tail gunner.

Boeing B-29A All Superfortress bombers built by the Boeing Renton factory between January 1944 and May 1946 were designated B-29A, although their specification and performance was similar to that of aircraft from the other three factories built under the plain B-29 designation. The principal difference was the method of wing construction which added an extra foot to the span of the Renton machines. On the B-29A a stub centre-section was used and the wing built up of seven sections compared with six in the integral method used by the other manufacturers. Only three instead of four fuel tanks were fitted in the B-29A centre section and resulted in a slightly reduced fuel capacity. Major changes were fuel tanks in the wing centre section and the removal of de-icers with the B-29A-5-BN; improved engine cooling and lubrication with the B-29A-10-BN; and the introduction of the four-gun turret, pneumatically operated bomb bay doors and the elimination of the cannon on the B-29A-20-BN. All told 1,119 B-29s were built.

Specification B-29A Power: as B-29. Wing span: 142 ft 3 in. Wing area: 1,738 sq ft. Fuselage length: 99 ft. Empty weight: 71,360 lb. General combat weight: 135,000 lb with 12,000 lb bombs. Normal bomb load for 1,600-mile radius mission was 5,000 lb at high altitude. With weight reduction a 12,000 lb load was possible over the same distance. Maximum bomb load 20,000 lb. Bomb accommodation as B-29. Built-in fuel tankage was 9,288 U.S. gallons including semi-permanent bomb bay tanks. Maximum range at optimum combat altitude of 25,000 ft was 4,000 miles. Maximum ferry range was 6,000 miles. Practical radius of action 1,800 miles. Time to 20,000 ft at 11,000 lb gross was 38 minutes and service ceiling was approximately 33,000 ft. Normal combat cruise speed range 200–220 mph. Armament and crew as B-29.

Boeing B-29B The need to improve the B-29's payload brought weight reduction measures in combat units and a request for similarly 'stripped down' models from production centres. In consequence Bell Atlanta produced a specialised model designated B-29B from January 1945. The General Electric fire-control system was omitted with all power turrets, leaving only the tail armament, although provision was made for two 0.50 guns to be installed and operated manually in the mid-fuselage side blisters. Other eliminations reduced the weight to a point where the payload could be increased by 4,000 lb over earlier B-29s. In practice the B-29B was able to carry even larger loads through operating at lower altitudes for optimum fuel consumption. Intended for low-altitude night missions the aircraft were fitted with the new AN/APQ-7 Eagle radar which produced a high relief ground scan image. A total of 311 B-29Bs were built, January to September 1945, and most were assigned to the 315th BW.

Specification of B-29B Power, wing span, wing area and fuselage length as B-29. Empty weight: 69,000 lb. General war loaded weight: 137,000 lb with 18,000 lb bombs. Normal bomb load for a 1,600-mile radius mission was 18,000 lb at 10,000 ft. Maximum bomb load 20,000 lb but with mixed incendiary load was 22,800 lb. Built-in fuel tankage 6,988 U.S. gallons (bomb-bay tanks eliminated). Maximum range at 10,000 ft was 4,200 miles with fuel and 18,000 lb bombs. Radius of action 1,800 miles. Time to 20,000 ft was 33 minutes at 110,000 lb gross and the service ceiling 32,000 ft. Maximum speed 364 mph at 25,000 ft. Normal cruise speed 210-225 mph. Armament: two or three 0.50-in machine guns in tail turret. Provision for two 0.50-in guns to be fired from mid-fuselage cabin. Crew seven or eight – as B-29 less three gunners.

Armament and Ordnance

BOMBS
Eighty different types of bomb were used by the AAF during World War II of which fifteen were commonly carried by the heavy bombers. The early B-17s were designed to use only the five main General Purpose (GP) high-explosive bombs available to the Air Corps: 100, 300, 600, 1,100 and 2,000 lb types. True weights of these bombs, fused and finned, was between 20 and 30 lb more than the classified weight, but in the case of the 300 lb type, 15 lb less. Classified weights of later bomb types were also rarely true weights and individual bombs also varied slightly.

High Explosive The early GP bombs were superseded by a new series during the late 'thirties and early 'forties classified as 100, 250, 500, 1,000, 2,000 and 4,000 lb. These were the predominant types used in the last two years of the war against both European and Pacific enemies. B-17s and B-24s delivered large quantities of all sizes except the 4,000 lb bomb, although this could be carried on external wing racks on short-range missions but there is no record of this being attempted. The 4,000 lb GP could be carried

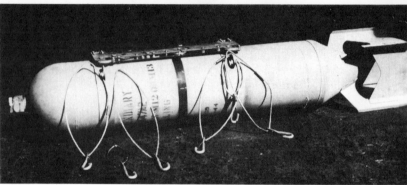

M44 1,000 lb
GP bomb
suspended from
external racks on a
303rd BG B-17F.

M34 2,000 lb GP
bombs in the bomb
dump at Bury St
Edmunds, England.

M47A2 incendiary
with shackles for
stowage in B-29
bomb bay.

internally by the B-29 and 1,220 were dropped on Japan by aircraft operating from the Mariannas during the last six months of the war. External
racks on B-17s and B-24s were little used because of range restrictions. B-17s
in England were fitted with them in the summer of 1943 to carry two 500 or
1,000 lb bombs on Channel coast attacks. GP bombs could be fused for
demolition or penetration. In the widely used 1,000 lb bomb, 435 lb was steel
casing and 530 lb explosive charge. In the 2,000 lb GP, 56 per cent of the
content was high explosive and in the 4,000 lb GP 77.4 per cent.

A 1,600 lb armour-piercing bomb was supplied to the 8th AF for use
against concrete and other hard structures in 1944, and 1,122 were expended.

Both 8th and 15th AF made use of bombs supplied by their Allies. B-17s
operating from shuttle bases in Russia used 1,645 Soviet 225 kilo bombs
(approximately 550 lb). The largest bombs used by the AAF during the
war were the special concrete-piercing rocket-boosted types of British design
and manufacture weighing 4,500 lb. These were used exclusively by 8th AF
B-17s as no RAF aircraft could accommodate them internally nor had suitable external racks. Rocket bombs were used against submarine and other

formidable structures on the enemy's coast during the early months of 1945, each B-17 carrying a bomb on each wing rack.

Incendiary The Air Corps showed little interest in incendiary devices during the inter-war years and did not develop suitable types for use in heavy bombers until 1940. Early examples, based on German and British magnesium types, were classified as 2 lb each and of the three variants, that having a steel case (to economise in magnesium) was the first used by the AAF, 120 being packed into a 250 lb cluster. Clusters facilitated stowage in aircraft bomb bays and allowed a close concentration of hits, for after falling free of the aircraft the cluster casing automatically burst to release individual bombs.

The standard small magnesium based incendiaries for incorporation in clusters were the 2 lb M52 and 4 lb M50. Both had hexagonal, cored, magnesium alloy bodies with hollow, sheet steel tails and contained a thermate burning composition and an igniting charge. The M50 also had a fuse mechanism and a blunt, cast-iron nose. These bombs burned for six to eight minutes at temperatures of 2,300°F. Clusters supplied to the 8th AF in 1943 were 100 lb (containing 34 × 4 lb M-50s) and 500 lb (containing 110 × 4 lb M50s). These proved unsatisfactory for high-altitude use being non-aimable and opening shortly after release, scattering individual incendiaries over a wide area with generally ineffective results. The M17 cluster, introduced in Europe in January 1944, was aimable and had a primacord charge time-fused to burst the cluster 5,000 feet from the ground achieving an intense concentration of hits. This 500 lb type containing 110 × 4 lb M50s was the main cluster used by 8th and 15th AFs. The M17 was also extensively used in B-29 raids on Japan but here a smaller cluster of 228 lb, the M19, containing 38 × 6 lb M69 jellied-oil bombs, predominated. The M69 was the standard jellied-oil based incendiary for use in clusters and had a 50-yard spread on impact. Clusters formed about a third of the total incendiary tonnage used against Germany and more than a third of that against Japan. Larger individual incendiary devices made up the total and until 1944 these were usually the 250 lb British oil-filled type. In the autumn of 1943 first use was made in Europe of an American developed incendiary with a petroleum-based filling. Shortage of magnesium and deficiencies in existing incendiaries prompted the U.S. Army's Chemical Warfare Service to experiment with petroleum mixtures which were found to burn longer and give better fire spread. A petrol, crude latex, caustic soda and coconut oil mix was the filling for the first production type, the M47, classified as 70 lb. This was superseded by the 100 lb M47A2 containing jellied-oil giving an impact spread of 40 yards. The M47A2 had a thin-walled steel cylindrical body, 49 inches long and eight inches in diameter and weighed 26 lb empty. The M47A1 used the same case but the filling included 93 lb of white phosphorus. The M47A2 was used in larger numbers by the strategic bombers than any other type of incendiary. Only limited use was made of the white phosphorus variant in the Pacific war but this type was extensively used against Germany in the last six months of hostilities.

The largest individual incendiary was the 500 lb M76, the 'pyrotechnic gel bomb' which had a special mixture of jellied-oil, heavy oil, petrol, magnesium powder and sodium nitrate. Exceptionally difficult to extinguish, the M76 saw only limited use in Europe but with the M47A2 was dropped in large numbers during the great fire raids on Japanese cities in 1945.

Aimable incendiary clusters containing 38 × M69 incendiaries each, stowed in a XXI BC B-29. An M26 cluster of M41 fragmentation bombs is included in the load to deter enemy fire-fighting teams.

Large petroleum jelly – napalm – bombs were made by filling fighter aircraft drop tanks with the mixture. Officially known as Class C-Fire bombs, B-17s and B-24s used the 108 U.S. gallon composition paper tanks, six per aircraft, in a few specialised missions against German strong-points on the coast of France during April 1945.

Fragmentation Anti-personnel bombs generally used by the heavies in saturation bombings of enemy troop concentrations in forward areas. These were large individual types, designed to fracture into small shrapnel on impact, and clusters of smaller anti-personnel bombs which were scattered in close proximity. The M81 260 lb individual type was almost exclusively the size employed by heavy bombers in the Pacific and predominantly that used in Europe. Most popular fragmentation cluster was the 128 lb M1 type (6 × 20 lb M41) in both theatres, although in Europe 540 lb types were used towards the end of hostilities.

Controllable Bombs A few stand-off bombs were developed by the AAF with the aims of great accuracy and avoidance of anti-aircraft defences. Small wings and empenage fitted to a 2,000 lb GP M34 bomb was the basis of the GB-1 glide bomb launched from the external wing racks of B-17s.

xperimental combat trials by the 8th AF during the spring of 1944 were bandoned due to the general inaccuracy of this weapon. The Azon Bomb, xperimentally used by 8th and 15th AF units during the same period, eatured a 1,000 lb or 2,000 lb GP with movable fins linked to a radio eceiver. After release, a flare in the tail ignited and kept it in view of the ombardier who controlled the bomb's movements in azimuth via a radio eceiver. Abandoned in Europe owing to the danger from flak, the controlling ircraft having to operate at reduced altitudes, the Azon bomb achieved ome success with B-24 units in the CBI theatre. GB-4 was something of a narriage of GB-1 with the Azon bomb and GB-8 was a further development f this glide bomb controlled visually through television. Both types were xperimentally launched from 8th AF B-17s in the closing months of the European conflict but proved technically unreliable and inaccurate.

Sea Mines Mines delivered by 20th AF Superfortresses in the blockade of Japanese home waters were U.S. Navy developments. Two sizes, 1,000 lb nd 2,000 lb, were used in nearly equal amounts during the campaign with verage B-29 bomb loads of 12,000 and 14,000 lb respectively. Mines were of nixed detonation types; magnetic, acoustic, pressure-magnetic and low requency acoustic. Delivery was by parachute from heights up to 8,000 ft.

GUNS

In contrast to other World War II combatants who favoured rifle-alibre machine guns or cannon, the standard defensive weapon on all U.S. ombers was the 0.50-in calibre Browning machine gun. Advantages over the 0.30-in weapon were a higher muzzle velocity and greater range, giving pene-ration of virtually any part of an attacking aircraft, including the engine at up to 800 yds. Fire from the smaller gun lost its effectiveness rapidly after 500 yards. The 'Point Fifty' model used in both turret and flexible mounts was the 0.50-in calibre M-2. It weighed 64 lb and was 57 in long. Muzzle velocity was 2,810 ft per second for an extreme range of 7,200 yds (the point at which forward travel terminated) and effective range against aircraft to approximately 1,200 yds. Rate of fire was 800 rounds per minute. A round of ammunition was 5.47 in long and weighed 1.71 oz. Principal types of round used in gun belts were armour piercing (identified by black painted ip), AP incendiary (silver) and tracer (red). Tracer had a chemical that gnited leaving the breech and gave the illusion of a stream of fire, its use being for observing the direction of aim and deterring enemy attacks through psychological effect.

The 0.30-in calibre Browning was similar in design to the larger gun. Used in early B-17s and B-24s for nose defence, the weapon was light enough for a man to move between socket locations in the nosepiece. Dispensed with in both Europe and Pacific theatres by early 1943, the 0.30-in calibre M-2 weighed 21 lb and was 40 in long. Muzzle velocity was 2,600 ft per second and extreme range 1,800 yds. Rate of fire was 1,350 rounds per minute. A single round of ammunition was 3.34 in long and weighed 2.1 ounces.

The B-29 was originally fitted with a 20 mm cannon for tail defence. This weapon was the 20 mm M-2B type weighing 102 lb and being some 94 in long, Muzzle velocity was 2,850 ft per second, extreme range 5,500 yds (effective range about 700 yds) and rate of fire 650 rounds per minute.

Armourers
assembling 0.50-in
belt ammunition
and feeding it
through a re-
positioning machine
to minimise
jamming. In this
case there are nine
rounds of armour
piercing to one of
tracer.

The Martin power
turret on a B-24D
featured a reflector
sight. The gunner
had a ⅜in sheet
of armour plate for
protection.

Specialised Equipment

GUNSIGHTS

Ring and bead sights were fitted to 0.50-in hand-held guns although
some B-17E and B-24D aircraft did have reflector sights which were
discarded as unsatisfactory. Optical and, later, computing type sights
were used in turrets and gave superior aim. The N-6 optical sight was used
in power turrets and N-8 in the hand-manipulated 'Cheyenne' tail turret of
B-17s. N model optical sights could also be installed on flexible guns.
The K-15 computing sight, which allowed accurate deflection shooting, was
fitted in some power turrets on B-17s and B-24s during the last few months of
hostilities.

AN/APG-5, a radar ranging device designed to supply range information
to lead computing sights in turrets, was experimentally fitted to a few bombers in Europe in March/April 1945. B-29 computing sights were an integral
part of the General Electric fire-control system.

BOMBSIGHTS

The bombsight used in high-altitude precision attacks was the Norden
M series, the M-7 being standard in B-17s and B-24s during the last year
of hostilities, Classified secret throughout most of the war, the Norden
was a highly sophisticated instrument which computed information on

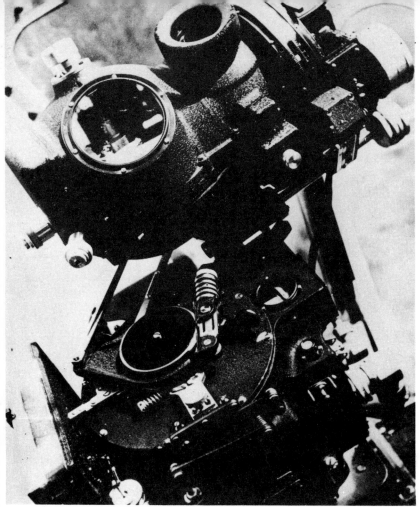

bomb ballistics, trail, ground speed and drift fed in by the bombardier. Through a telescopic attachment on the sight the bombardier established range and compensated for deflection to synchronise the instrument, the bombs then released automatically when the aircraft reached the point computed by the sight. Automatic Flight Control Equipment, which enabled the bombardier to control lateral movement of the aircraft through his adjustments of the sight, was incorporated in B-17s, B-24s and B-29s.

The D-8 sight was sometimes installed in B-17s and B-24s in lieu of the Norden for medium- and low-altitude operations.

BLIND BOMBING DEVICES

Several British radio/radar aids were adopted by the AAF with the primary purpose of enabling bombing to be carried out when targets were shrouded by cloud. A few of these were developed by U.S. laboratories to produce more sophisticated models.

Gee British navigational device involving special aircraft radio receiver working on signals pulsated by three ground stations. Limited to a range of some 400 miles. Used by 8th AF in bad weather harassing raids (Moling) experiments during winter 1942-1943 and later widely installed in B-17s and B-24s purely as navigational aid.

Oboe British technique involving two ground stations but in contrast to Gee an aircraft's position was assessed at the ground stations which operated on re-radiation of radar signals directed at the aircraft. Range limited to 280 miles. Limited pathfinder use by 8th AF in winter 1943–1944.

H2S: 'Stinkey' British airborne radar providing ground contour image on radar scope screen (cathode ray tube). Revolving scanner antennae in radome situated under nose of B-17s and in position usually occupied by ball turret on B-24s. Used by 8th AF on some twenty aircraft August 1943–March 1944 for pathfinder purposes.

AN/APS-15: 'H2X': 'Mickey' U.S. developed version of H2S. Standard bombing through overcast device for 8th and 15th AFs. Radome located under nose of twelve B-17s with pre-production models, but all production sets located in position usually occupied by ball turret on B-17 and B-24. Scope and operator positioned in fuselage adjacent to radome in both types. Semi-retractable on B-17s and fully retractable on B-24.

G-H Development of Gee giving more precise fixes to aircraft. Used by 8th AF from January 1944 for short-range missions to targets generally near the enemy coastline.

Micro-H A further development of the Gee system utilising ground stations signals but combined with H2X for bombing. Micro-H beacons were established in continental Europe in autumn of 1944 and used for short-range missions chiefly to Ruhr area.

AN/APQ-7 'Eagle' Developed to replace AN/APS-15 types. The antennae housed in a 16-in wide aerofoil shaped section under the fuselage swept from side to side through approximately 60 degrees, the beam being formed in the forward path of the aircraft in contrast to the revolving scanners of AN/APS-15 which swept through 360 degrees. A much higher frequency was used with AN/APQ-7 giving a clearer presentation of ground images on the radar scope. Fitted as standard to B-29Bs used by 20th AF. Experimental combat trials on B-24s of 8th and 15th AF in the early spring of 1945.

AN/APQ-13 Development of AN/APS-15 ground scanning radar installed in B-29s. Retractable radome located between the two bomb bays.

RADIO COUNTERMEASURES EQUIPMENT
To combat the development of increasingly efficient defensive enemy radar devices, the AAF adopted some of the equipment used successfully by British night bombers. A special RCM unit operated with the 8th AF but during the latter half of 1944 installations of some RCM items were made to regular bombing aircraft.

Chaff Equivalent of British 'Window'. Metallic foil strips dropped in vast quantities on approach to a target to saturate radar screens. Effectively used by the strategic air forces in Europe from late 1943 until the end of hostilities and also by the 20th AF in operations over Japan. A dispenser unit

(A-1) fitted in late production B-17s and B-24s.

AN/APQ-9 'Carpet' A transmitter for barrage jamming technique operating on frequencies of German fire-control radars. Installed selectively in B-17s and B-24s from the autumn of 1943 but approximately three-quarters of the aircraft in the 8th and 15th AFs had this equipment by the end of hostilities.

AN/APT-2 and AN/APT-5 Transmitters for spot-jamming German radar transmissions fitted extensively to both 8th and 15th AF bombers during final year of war in Europe.

Crew Equipment

Oxygen The oxygen system in B-17s and B-24s was originally the continuous flow type where individual crew members adjusted the valve governing the amount of oxygen reaching the face mask. The superior demand-type system came into use during 1942 and had replaced the earlier system in both bombers by the end of the following year. Developed by Dr R. Lovelace and the Aero Medical Laboratory, Wright Field, it was fully automatic and increased the oxygen content of the air supply as an aircraft gained altitude, maintaining ground level value. It also only functioned when a man was inhaling and automatically adjusted to the individual speed of breathing. Oxygen was stored in several lightweight low-pressure bottles to nullify the effects of battle damage. Walk-around bottles were carried in the aircraft for use when crew members had to move from their normal stations. The smallest type held about five minutes' supply and the large type about one and a half hours' supply. A bomber crew usually went on to oxygen at 10,000 ft.

Masks which closely fitted face contours had built-in microphones for inter-crew or radio communication. Uncomfortable and often obstructed by icing, the standard A-10 mask was revised early in 1943 to eliminate these troubles. By the following year the improved A-14 mask had become standard in both 8th and 15th AFs.

Clothing At 25,000 ft temperatures were normally between − 30 deg F and − 50 deg F over Europe necessitating special clothing to keep aircrew warm. This consisted of long woollen underwear over which was worn normal uniform trousers and shirt, an electrically heated flying suit, and finally an alpaca suit or fleece-lined leather jacket and trousers. Fleece-lined leather helmets encompassing earphones were supplied for head protection. Felt or fleece-lined flying boots were worn over various combinations of wool, rayon and silk socks, while hands were protected by leather gloves over silk. Both flying boots and outer gloves could be electrically heated. Full electrically heated clothing was usually only used by gunners in the rear of the aircraft who were exposed at open-waist windows to severe draughts. The early electric suit known as model F-1, was a one-piece blue coloured garment wired in series. The later F-2 suit consisted of elastic grip jacket and trousers with a button-in electric liner. The final F-3 type was an auxiliary garment designed simply to carry the electric wiring and had to be used as part of a complete outfit under an improved alpaca suit. Individual variations were numerous and in summer additional clothing was carried in a

Gunners with fleece-lined and plain leather flying jackets over heated suits, leather helmets, parachute harness and Mae West life-savers. Two ground crew men at right also wear fleece-lined jackets.

B-17 gunner putting on an F-1 electrically heated flying suit.

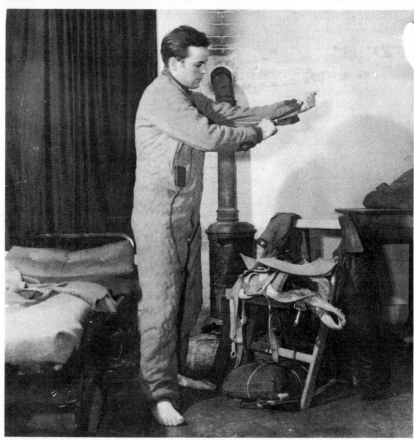

bomber to don in flight at higher altitudes. Goggles, usually tinted, were worn for eye protection by waist gunners and often by other members of the crew for combat protection against fire and flying debris. B-29 crews in pressurised and heated compartments did not need heavy clothing although some was carried in case of emergencies.

Body Armour 'Flak vests' were originally developed in the U.K. by 8th AF surgeons in co-operation with a British manufacturer. In 1943 it was established that causes of combat wounds were 40 per cent flak shrapnel, 40 per cent 20 mm shrapnel, 10 per cent machine gun bullets and 10 per cent fragments of aircraft structure blasted by shell hits. Thin steel-plate armour, made flexible by using small overlapped panels, in a containing canvas garment, was found to protect against 20 mm fragments and from distant flak burst shrapnel. The value of body armour was established by the fact that two-thirds of men hit by missiles or fragments while wearing flak jackets escaped injury, and only 8.2 per cent of the remainder were killed. Standard body armour produced in the U.S. from 1944 consisted of four main types: M-1 vest with armoured front and back panels, weighing 18 lb 2 oz; M-2 vest, armoured in the front only and intended for men occupying armour-plate seats – weight approximately 9 lb; M-3 tapered apron, for men in sitting position where lower part of body is unprotected – weight 4 lb 12 oz; and M-4 full apron, protecting all frontal area of body, and usually worn by gunners – weight 7 lb 8 oz. U.S. infantry steel helmets were supplied for head protection but made it difficult to wear earphones. A special steel helmet incorporating earphones was supplied in the summer of 1944. Body armour and helmets were not donned until entering hostile airspace.

Personal Safety Equipment Yellow 'Mae West' inflatable life preservers were worn on the chest over all flying clothes. When inflated they could support an airman in water in full flying clothes. Originally supplied by the British in European and Mediterranean theatres.

Parachutes originally used by most 8th AF heavy bomber crews were chest packs from British sources. These had silk canopies and by early 1944 were being superseded by nylon chest packs from U.S. production. Early U.S. made parachutes were chiefly backpack type found difficult to don quickly in an emergency and impeded movement. Chest packs were positioned adjacent to crew positions and could be quickly snapped onto the parachute harness worn over flying clothes. As all parachutes were heavy and made movement difficult they were not generally worn until an emergency occurred.

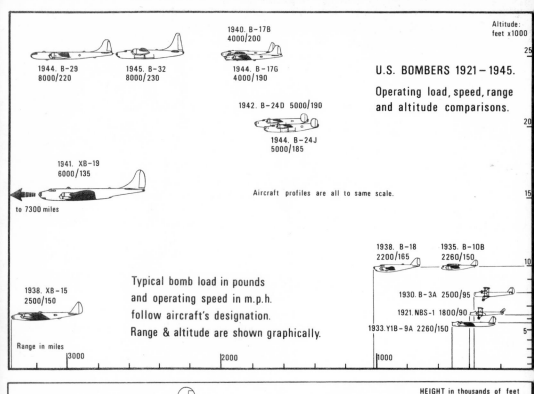

1944. B-29
8000/220

1945. B-32
8000/230

1940. B-17B
4000/200

1944. B-17G
4000/190

U.S. BOMBERS 1921-1945.

Operating load, speed, range
and altitude comparisons.

Altitude:
feet x1000

25

1942. B-24D 5000/190

1944. B-24J
5000/185

20

1941. XB-19
6000/135

Aircraft profiles are all to same scale.

15

to 7300 miles

1938. B-18
2200/165

1935. B-10B
2260/150

10

1938. XB-15
2500/150

Typical bomb load in pounds
and operating speed in m.p.h.
follow aircraft's designation.
Range & altitude are shown graphically.

1930. B-3A 2500/95
1921. NBS-1 1800/90
1933. Y1B-9A 2260/150

5

Range in miles

|3000

|2000

|1000

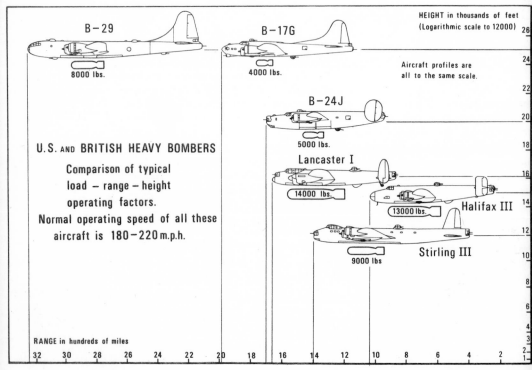

B-29

B-17G

HEIGHT in thousands of feet
(Logarithmic scale to 12000)
26

8000 lbs.

4000 lbs.

Aircraft profiles are
all to the same scale.

24

22

B-24J

20

5000 lbs.

18

Lancaster I

U.S. AND BRITISH HEAVY BOMBERS

Comparison of typical
load – range – height
operating factors.
Normal operating speed of all these
aircraft is 180–220 m.p.h.

14000 lbs.

16

13000 lbs.

Halifax III

14

Stirling III

12

9000 lbs

10

8

6

RANGE in hundreds of miles

4

32   30   28   26   24   22   20   18   16   14   12   10   8   6   4   2

2
1

7. Training

Prior to 1939 Air Corps training was insignificant in both size and scope, with specialised bombardment instruction usually given within operational units. With the prospect of war, measures were taken to expand flying training facilities but as late as 1941 there were still no formal training courses for air gunners and many ground duties. Under pressure of war the AAF established an extremely proficient and comprehensive training organisation; by early 1942 this was being conducted in two commands, Technical Training and Flying Training, merging in July 1943 into AAF Training Command. Some idea of the development of this organisation can be gauged from the fact that whereas only 966 men were under flying training instruction in September 1939, four years later there were nearly 224,000. At the same date 125,000 men and women were receiving various forms of technical training.

INDIVIDUAL TRAINING

All aviation cadet recruits were given a 5-week introductory military course involving physical and aptitude tests to ascertain suitability for training as pilot, bombardier or navigator.

Pilot Following the 5-week introductory course, a 10-week course at pre-flight school or replacement centre followed for physical and academic training. Then a 10-week course at primary flying school with 70 hours in basic trainers. This was followed by a course of the same length and flying hours using more advanced training aircraft at a basic flying school. Here, on the basis of choice, instructors' reports and AAF requirements, trainee pilots were classified for the next stage, either single or multi-engined advanced training. Those selected for bomber or transport duties then spent 10 weeks at an advanced flying training school with 70 hours on twin-engined aircraft (AT-9, AT-10, AT-17 or AT-24 types). Graduates were given wings and either appointed Flight Officers* or commissioned 2nd Lieutenant. (Physical failures were offered commissions in various ground posts.) Pilots destined for heavy bomber units next spent a further 10 weeks at a transition flying training school utilising 4-engine aircraft, for 105 hours' experience in B-17s or B-24s. Future B-29 pilots had 44 hours in B-17s and 126 in B-29s at a transitional school. Graduates were then sent to Operational Training Units, either B-17, B-24 or B-29. In 1943 the cost of training a B-17 or B-24 pilot was $25,000 and took 55 weeks on average.

* Flight Officer was an appointment for a flying training cadet who graduated but did not qualify for a commission.

Navigator Ten weeks preflight school, 6 weeks at gunnery school (as in B-17 and B-24 both bombardier and navigator were required to use armament), 20 weeks at navigation school and 104 hours in the air on practical navigation and 782 hours classroom instruction on pilotage, instruments, radio navigation aids, meteorology, dead reckoning, codes and signals. Graduates commissioned and assigned to unit training. Navigators selected for B-29 units or specialised B-17/B-24 operations took a 12-week course in bombardment before going to units.

Bombardier Ten weeks at preflight school, 6 weeks gunnery school, 20 weeks bombardier school with 120 hours practical training at bomb sights in AT-11 and 718 hours in classroom covering 388 hours on bombing theory and technical study of Norden and 330 hours navigational training including related subjects – meteorology, radar aids, code practice and recognition. Course graduates appointed Flight Officers or commissioned 2nd Lieutenant before passing on to unit training.

Air Gunner Career air gunners were all enlisted men (non-commissioned). After a 5-week introductory military training, those selected for these duties took a 6-week course at gunnery school. The course covered use of weapons and their operation, ballistics, turret operation and maintenance, and aircraft and ship recognition. The practical part included ground firing of flexible weapons and turret operation both from stationary and moving bases; air to ground and air to air firing, the latter at towed targets. More sophisticated gunnery training was introduced in 1944 with air to air cine-gun camera 'firing' and remote-control turret operation. To develop 'lead' a considerable amount of 'skeet' shooting was done by all gunners using 0.22 rifles, 12 bore shotguns as well as 0.30 and 0.50 weapons. The same or similar six-week course was taken by officers with a gunnery requirement.

Radio Operator Enlisted men. Following introductory training, a 20-week course in radio operation and repair, followed by a 6-week gunnery course.

Flight Engineer On B-17 and B-24 the flight engineer was an enlisted man and also served as top-turret gunner. After initial training, a 27-week course in aircraft maintenance and inspection was undertaken at a flight engineering school followed by the 6-week gunnery course. B-29 flight engineers were originally enlisted men but in late 1944 it was decided future trainees would be commissioned and have the ability to serve as a third pilot in an emergency. Non-commissioned flight engineers with operational units were unaffected by this decision. The more extensive training period for B-29 flight engineers consisted of 10 weeks preflight school and 19 weeks flight engineers school. Graduates were appointed Flight Officer or commissioned 2nd Lieutenant.

Radar Observer In the spring of 1944 a 10-week course for radar observers was introduced by AAF Training Command. Students were usually men with previous bombardier/navigator training which were necessary skills in many blind bombing techniques.

Ground Technicians Engineering courses for heavy bomber support were generally 29 weeks, armament 23 weeks, communications 20 to 44 weeks. By mid-1945 there were eighty different types of ground-duty courses.

The foregoing details of the training pattern for the intensive 1943–1944 period were subject to considerable variation. In 1942 the urgent need for trained personnel in combat areas curtailed some training periods.

UNIT AND CREW TRAINING

During the pre-war expansion period most of the bombardment groups in the continental U.S.A. became, in effect, operational training units (OTU). New groups were formed by taking cadres from an established group and supplementing the nucleus with graduates from training schools. Air and ground personnel trained together, initially under the auspices of the parent group. The pattern in use by mid-1942 involved three phases, the first formative stage brought crews together and assessed individual abilities within each team. In the second phase, usually conducted after a move to another base, formation flying and teamwork predominated. The final phase, often with squadrons detached to different airfields, was in simulated operations. Unit training was planned to take 90 days, but in practice this varied. Heavy bomber OTUs were concentrated under the 2nd AF during 1942 and 1943.

An important development was the AAF School of Applied Tactics at Orlando, Florida, opened in March 1943 to give specialised training to key personnel of new groups. Approximately 150 officers and men were detached during its first phase for a 30-day course. Instruction covered the latest combat tactics and technical background in the war zones. The final 2 weeks were spent in operating under simulated combat conditions from the three bomber airfields controlled by the school. These specialised courses for key men helped raise the general standard of training in new units. The 390th BG assigned to the 8th AF in July 1943 was the first heavy bomber group to be processed by AAFSAT.

A total of twenty-five groups acted as OTU and RTU (Replacement Training Units) during the period December 1941 to April 1944, most having gone over to RTU work by the end of 1943. RTUs were distributed among all four home air forces at that time although the largest concentration remained in the 2nd AF. A change of status was effected on 1st April 1944 when all training groups were inactivated and training continued on a station basis. The only remaining OTUs were for B-29s under the 16th and 17th Bombardment Training Wings of the 2nd AF, which also conducted B-29 RTU training. Replacements for bomber units in combat theatres were usually complete crews although they were often dispersed on reaching a combat unit. RTU training closely paralleled OTU training in that it was divided into three overlapping phases and took 90 days.

Further training programmes were carried out in the combat theatres where Combat Crew Replacement Units were set up, first in the U.K. and later in North Africa and Pacific war theatres. These were basically finishing schools where replacement personnel were indoctrinated in respective theatre procedures. Once committed to combat every bomber group set up a training section with the intention of improving skills. Lead crew training was particularly intensive. These crews were selected from group combatants exhibiting expertise and given a 6- to 7-week course before flying a group or squadron lead. On average lead crews flew one combat mission to every five training missions and they undertook ground school instruction every day.

8. Command Personalities

A selection of Army Air Force's commanders who influenced the development of the strategic bombing weapon, doctrine or operations.

General Henry H. Arnold

Born Gladwyne, Pa, 25th June 1886. Graduated from USMA and commissioned in the infantry on 14th June 1907. After service in the Philippines was assigned to the SC in April 1911, where he became one of the U.S. Army's first qualified pilots (Licence No. 29), having received instruction at Dayton, Ohio, in June that year. He later became a flying instructor in the Aviation School set up in the SC. Arnold saw no service in Europe during World War I, his administrative ability gaining him the post of Chief of Information Service, Aviation Division, SC in 1917 and later Assistant Director, Office of Military Aeronautics. Commanded Rockwell Fd, Cal, in 1919. A friend and admirer of Mitchell, Arnold took a more cautious path to achieve similar ideals. In 1925 his flair for the written and spoken word gained him position of Chief, Information Division, Office C of AC. Entered CGSS and graduated in June 1929. Commanded 1st Wing at March Fd, Cal, from November 1933 to March 1936, and while holding this command led a flight of B-10 bombers to Alaska gaining the Mackay Trophy award. Promoted Brigadier General (temporary) in February 1935 and appointed Assistant Chief of AC. With the death of Major General Westover, Arnold became C of AC in September 1938. Became the Army's Deputy C of S for Air in October 1940 and given the overall command of the Army's air arm in June 1941, with the creation of the AAF, first US Chief of the AAF and with the reorganisation of Army command he became CG, AAF on 9th March 1942. Promoted Lieutenant General (temporary) December 1941 and General (temporary) in March 1943. Received a 5th star in December 1944, first air officer to achieve this rank.

Awards: DFC, DSM and AM.

A notable writer, his book *Global Mission* (1949) reflects his receptive approach to the various aspects of airpower and an intense determination to succeed. Died 15th January 1950.

General Carl A. Spaatz

Born 28th June 1891 at Boyertown, Pa. Graduated from USMA West Point, and commissioned in the infantry June 1914. Stationed a year in Hawaii from October 1914. On return to U.S.A. received pilot training at San Diego, Cal. Assigned to 1st AS as pilot on Mexican border during 1916. Promoted Captain May 1917 and sent to France where he commanded the AS training base at Issoudon. In 1918 spent a period with 2nd PG and shot down three enemy a/c. Promoted Major 1920 and commanded Kelly Fd, Texas, between October 1920 and February 1921. Became Air Officer 8th Corps Area and then, in November 1921, assumed command of 1st PG, holding this command at Ellington Fd, Texas, and Selfridge Fd, Mich, until September 1924. Major Spaatz then entered the ASTS at Langley, Va, and after graduating in June 1925 went to Washington for staff duties in the Office of C of the AS. In January 1929 Spaatz and his crew accomplished an air-refuelled flight lasting six days. In the following May he was assigned to command the 7th BG at Rockwell Fd, Cal, and in October 1931 became CO of the controlling 1st Wing at March Fd. In June 1933 he returned to Washington as C of AC, Training and Operations Division, following which he attended the CGSS. Promoted

ieutenant Colonel early in 1936 and in June assigned to GHQ AF, Langley Fd,
.a.

Early in 1939 he returned to Washington to take up the appointment of Assist-
nt Executive Officer to the C of AC. Promoted Colonel that November he was
ent to the U.K. in the spring of 1940 as a special military observer. On return, in
October, he became Arnold's assistant and was promoted Brigadier General.
During 1941 Spaatz was head of the Plans Division and later became Chief of
Air Staff. With war he was made CO of AAFCC and promoted Major General in
anuary 1942. Detailed to organise forces for a European campaign he then
ssumed command of the 8th AF in the U.K. in July. In November 1942 he went to
North Africa, commanding the 12th AF and the NAAF with promotion to Lieu-
enant General in March 1943. Later in 1943 he became Deputy Commander of the
MAAF, returning to the U.K. in January 1944 to become first commander of
USSTAF. Promoted General in March 1945 he returned to Washington in
une and was then despatched to Guam to form U.S. Strategic Air Forces Pacific.
Spaatz was present at all three WW2 unconditional surrender signings. Post-war he
became commander of the AAF in February 1946 and the first C of S of the new
USAF when founded in September 1947. Retired 30th June 1948. Deceased
14th June 1974.

Awards: DSC, DSM and 3 OLC, LM, DFC and many foreign decorations.

Lieutenant General Ira C. Eaker

Born 13th April 1896 at Llano, Texas. School teacher before obtaining a commission in the infantry in August 1917. Detached for flying training November
917. Pilot and Assistant Adjutant, Rockwell Fd, Cal, 1918–19. Served with 2nd
nd 3rd AS, Philippines, 1919–22, and on return to U.S. became CO of 5th AS
t Mitchel Fd, NY, 1922–23. Two university courses followed and up until 1932
Captain Eaker held Executive Officer assignments in Washington. During this
period he was also associated with technical evaluation and experimentation. In
927 he participated in a goodwill Pan American flight and was decorated by
three governments. Acted as chief pilot 1st–7th January 1929 during record
ndurance flight over Los Angeles where air-to-air refuelling was successfully
mployed. In 1933 he made the first 'blind' trans-continental flight of U.S.A.
Commanded 34th PS, 17th PG, in the mid-1930s and staff appointments in
Washington 1938–40. Collaborated with General Arnold in writing *Winged
Warfare, This Flying Game*. Executive Officer to Chief of Air Corps in 1940.
Commanded 20th FG at Hamilton Fd, Cal, from January to September 1941,
then spent a month in the U.K. as a special observer. Joined 1st AF HQ at Mitchel
Fd late 1941 and chosen to head an expeditionary bomber command destined for
the U.K. Reached the U.K. in February 1942 and assumed command of VIII BC
ater that month. Flew on the first 8th AF heavy bomber mission in August and
n December 1942 became the CG of 8th AF. Directed the 8th AF campaign
until January 1944 when he was transferred to the MTO to command the new
MAAF. Flew on the first 15th AF 'shuttle' mission to Russia in June 1944.
Remained overall Allied air commander in the MTO until the end of hostilities.
Deputy CG of the AAF after returning to the U.S.A., April 1945, holding this
office until his own retirement in June 1947. Prominent commentator on air
affairs for over 25 years during retirement.

Awards: DSM, SS, LM, DFC and OLC and numerous foreign decorations.

Lieutenant General Kenneth B. Wolfe

Born 12th August 1896 in Denver, Colorado. Enlisted as a private in the Army
n 1917 and was commissioned as a 2nd Lieutenant in the AS July 1918. Served as a
flying instructor before a technical appointment in 1919 as Engineering Officer

at a depot in Georgia. Promoted 1st Lieutenant in July 1920 and later served as Operations Officer with the 3rd PS at Clark Fd, Philippines. Reverted to technical work in 1930 when appointed Engineering Officer at Brooks, Texas, and Langley, Va. In 1931 he was assigned to the AC Material Division at Wright Fd, Dayton, as Chief of the Inspection Section, and for the next 12 years was associated with engineering and procurement matters. Wolfe was involved in experimental and testing projects at Wright Field and later served as an AC representative in liaison with aircraft manufacturers. In the spring of 1939 involved in the organisation of the Production Engineering Section of Material Command dealing with the complex problem of volume production of aircraft, and playing a notable part in arrangements for the expansion of B-17 and B-24 production. Later intimately involved in the B-29 project, heading the B-29 Liaison Committee formed in February 1942. With this appointment he was made a Brigadier General, the second promotion in two months. Wolfe organised 'B-29 Special Project' in April 1943 to speed production, overseeing flight testing, training crews and forming combat units. He prepared 'Air Plan for the Defeat of Japan' presented to Allied leaders at the Quebec meeting. In June 1943 Wolfe assumed command of the 58th BW with the first combat B-29 units. In November 1943 became the first commander of XXBC, conducting its initial operations in the CBI. In July 1944 was recalled to Washington to head Material Command, being promoted to Major General in November 1944 and returned to the familiar haunts of Wright Patterson. Post-war he commanded 5th AF in Japan from October 1945 to January 1948 when his experience was required for the post of Director of Procurement and Industrial Planning, Material Command. Retired as Lieutenant General in 1951, the last two years of his 33 years' service having been spent as Deputy C of S for Material, USAF HQ. Deceased 20th September 1971.

Awards: DFC and OLC.

Lieutenant General James H. Doolittle

Born 14th December 1896 at Alameda, Cal. Attended the University of California and enlisted as a flying cadet in the SC Reserve in October 1917. Commissioned 2nd Lieutenant in March 1918. In September 1922 made the first trans-continental flight in the U.S.A. Entered MIT in 1923 and received Master's and Doctor's degree in 1924 and 1925. In October 1925 won a Schneider Trophy contest. Resigned regular Army commission in February 1930 but remained on the reserve as a major. Made a number of record flights during the 1930s chiefly in racing aircraft. Member of Baker Board enquiry into the AC in 1934 and only civilian to advocate separation of AC from Army. Ordered to active duty in July 1940. Organised special strike force to bomb Tokyo during early 1942, carrying out the operation with B-25 bombers from carriers in the Pacific on 18th April 1942. Awarded the Medal of Honor for this action. Commanded 4th BW from June to August 1942 then sent to Europe as Commander 12th AF, taking this force to North Africa in November. At the end of February 1943 assumed command of XII BC which he relinquished in November 1943, moving to the U.K. to command of 8th AF. Remained CG 8th AF in U.K. until July 1945 and then in Pacific until September 1945. After retirement headed USAF Scientific Advisory Board for a number of years.

General Nathan F. Twining

Born 11th October 1897 at Monroe, Wisconsin. Joined the Oregon NG in 1916 and became a regular soldier in 1918, graduating as 2nd Lieutenant from USMA in November that year. Sent as an observer to the Occupational Army in Germany July 1919 and on return in September trained for service with an infantry regiment. Undertook pilot training in August 1923 and subsequently became an instructor, acting in this capacity until given an assignment with 18th PG in Hawaii in February 1929. During three years in Hawaii he held a number of posts including command of the 26th A Sq. On return to the U.S.A. 1st Lieutenant Twining served as a squadron commander in the 3rd AG and eventually group adjutant. In March 1935 he became Assistant Operations Officer, 3rd Wing at Barksdale Fd, La, and five months later entered the ACTS at Maxwell. A year later, on course completion, he entered the CGSC. Held various staff appointments during the five years to July 1942, latterly in the Operations Division, AAF HQ, where he was Assistant Executive to C of S, AAF. Promoted Brigadier General (temporary) in June 1942, he was sent to the South Pacific as C of S to the CG U.S. Army Forces in the South Pacific Area. Early 1943 as first commander of the 13th AF in New Caledonia, he skilfully directed operations of its few B-17 units in a most difficult logistical situation. He spent six days on a life raft when shot down in a B-17. On the 23rd July 1943 he was given the first joint air command in U.S. history with tactical control of U.S. Army, Navy and Marine units plus Commonwealth air units in the Solomon Island campaigns. Considered one of AAF's most promising commanders, Twining transferred to Europe in December 1943 to command the recently formed 15th AF and the Mediterranean Allied Strategic Air Forces. His record with the 15th AF brought a return to the Pacific and command of 20th AF when hostilities ceased in Europe, although less than two weeks of operations ensued when he took over. Post-war commands included AMC (December 1945 to October 1947), Alaskan Command (October 1947 to July 1950), Vice C of S USAF with temporary rank of General (October 1950 to June 1953) and C of S USAF (June 1953 to August 1957). Chairman of JC of S (August 1957 to September 1960) first USAF Commander to hold this office. General Twining retired 30th September 1960.

Awards: DSM and OLC, Navy DSM, LM and OLC, DFC, BS, AM and OLC. British KBE and many other foreign decorations.

Major General Haywood S. Hansell Jr

Born 1903. Flying training in the early 1920s. Member of the Air Corps aerobatic and demonstration team 1931–35. Instructor at ACTS in Air Force Section, 1935–1938. Graduated Army C & GS School, 1939. Chief, Strategic Intelligence Section, Office of Chief of AC, 1940. Chief, European Branch, Air War Plans Division, HQ AAF in 1941, being a member of the team that produced AWPD-1. Member of the Joint Strategic Committee, JCS, 1942. In summer 1942 promoted Brigadier General and sent to U.K. as Deputy Theatre Air Officer, ETO. Headed team producing AWPD-42. Commanded 3rd BW 8th AF from early December 1942 and the following month assumed command of the 1st BW, directing operations of B-17 groups until June 1943. Assigned as Deputy to C in C, AEAF, returning to Washington later in the year to serve on Joint Plans Committee, JCS. In April 1944 he became Deputy CS AAF and CS, 20th AF, directing B-29 operations. Assigned as CG, XXI BC, in August 1944 and moved to Mariannas with the B-29 force. Recalled to U.S.A. in January 1945 to direct B-29 training operations.

Major General Lawrence S. Kuter

Born 28th May 1905 at Rockford, Ill. Graduated from USMA, West Point, and commissioned in the artillery June 1927. Detailed for flying training in July 1929, graduating from Brooks and Kelly Fds, Texas. In June 1930 assigned to Langley Fd, Va, as Operations Officer 49th BS and of the parent 2nd BG in July 1933. Between February and June 1934 he was involved in the Army Air Mail operation in the eastern U.S.A., thereafter entering the ACTS at Maxwell Fd where, after graduating in spring 1935, he remained as a bombardment instructor. Promoted Captain, June 1937. In July 1939 assigned to the Operations and Training Division of the WD/GS in Washington. While in this he contributed to a num-

ber of Air Corps documents including the influential AWPD-1. Promoted Major (temporary) in December 1940. In November 1941 he was made Assistant Secretary WD/GS and received temporary promotion to Lieutenant Colonel in January 1942 and, less than a month later, to Brigadier General. In March he became Deputy C of S, HQ AAF and assigned to the 8th AF in the U.K. in October 1942 commanding the 1st BW until the end of the year. In January 1943 Brigadier General Kuter went to North Africa serving on Eisenhower's staff and becoming Deputy Commander, NAAF in April. Recalled to Washington in May 1943 he was designated Assistant Chief of AS for Plans. For two years he prepared the studies for and determined the means to implement operations against major objectives in all theatres; as Arnold's senior planning member he attended the JCS conferences at Quebec, Cairo and London, and represented Arnold at Malta and Yalta. Promoted to Major General (temporary) in February 1944. In May 1945 sent to the Mariannas as Deputy Commander, AAF, POA, to organise the U.S. Strategic Air Forces in the Pacific. Post-war commands included the Atlantic Division of ATC, MATS and, in November 1951, Deputy C of S, Personnel. Head of Air University, April 1953; and from June 1955, the FEAF – later PACAF – until July 1959.

Awards: DSM and OLC, LM, BS, French Legion of Honor, British OBE.

Major General Frederick L. Anderson Jr

Born 4th October 1905 at Kingston, NY. Graduated from USMA and commissioned 2nd Lieutenant in the Cavalry June 1928. Undertook flying instruction the following year, graduating at Kelly Fd, Texas, in September. Served with air units in the Philippines between 1930 and 1934. Entered the ACTS and in July 1940 became Director of Bombardment Instruction. In January 1942 became Deputy Director of Bombardment at AAF HQ. Promoted Brigadier General and sent to the U.K., commanding 3rd BW from February to April 1943. Became CO 4th BW in April 1943 and CG VIII BC in June. With the inactivation of VIII BC in January 1944 he became Deputy Commander for Operations at USSTAF.

Awards: SS, LM, DFC and AM.

General Curtis E. LeMay

Born 15th November 1906 at Columbus, Ohio. Graduated from Ohio State University with a degree in civil engineering. Accepted as a flying cadet in 1928, completing training in October 1929 at Kelly Field, Texas, and assigned to the 27th PS, 1st PG, at Selfridge Fd, Mich, in 1930 and received fighter assignments until 1937 when he went to the 2nd BG at Langley, Va, as Operations Officer, 49th BS. Took part in two record breaking flights by YB-17 Flying Fortress to South America acting as lead navigator. Navigator of XB-15 on 2,839-mile flight over Galapagos Islands on 9th May 1940. In January 1941 organised 7th BS (34th BG) when activated at Langley but in June was seconded to Ferrying Command to undertake pioneering flights to Africa in B-24s where he served as command navigator. Returned 34th BG in October 1941 and became Group Operations Officer. His advancement in bomber organisations now accelerated. In April 1942 he became Group Executive of fledgling 306th BG and in the following July commander of the equally raw 305th BG at Muroc, Cal. He took the 305th to the U.K. and entered combat in November 1942, his endeavours to improve bombing technique – notably the idea of lead crews – brought him promotion to Brigadier General and command of 8th AF's 4th BW (later 3rd BD) from July 1943 to June 1944. Returning to the U.S.A. he was promoted to Major General and sent to take over the XX BC in India where his handling of the troublesome B-29s earned transfer to the XXI BC in January 1945. Responsible for directing the successful strategic bombing of Japan, Major General LeMay was given Command of the

20th AF in July 1945 and became C of S, Strategic Air Forces, Pacific in early August. Post-war service included Deputy Commander of Research and Development at AAF HQ from December 1945 to October 1947; C in C USAFE in Germany from October 1947 to October 1948. C in C SAC October 1948 to June 1957, Vice C of S, USAF July 1957 to June 1961, and C of S, USAF, July 1961 to January 1965. Retired from USAF 1st February 1965.

Awards: DSC, DSM with 2 OLC, SS, DFC with 2 OLC, AM with 3 OLC, British DFC and other foreign decorations.

9. Operational Statistics

Heavy Bomber Units of the 8th Air Force
(*In order of entering combat*)

Bombardment Group	Bombardment Squadrons	Date Group Operational	A/c Type	Bombardment Wing
97 BG	340, 341, 342, 414	17 Aug 1942*	B-17	1 BW
301 BG	32, 352, 353, 419	5 Sep 1942*	B-17	1 BW
92 BG	325, 326, 327, 407	6 Sep 1942†	B-17	40 CBW
93 BG	328, 329, 330, 409	9 Oct 1942	B-24	20 CBW
306 BG	367, 368, 369, 423	9 Oct 1942	B-17	40 CBW
44 BG	66, 67, 68, 506	7 Nov 1942	B-24	14 CBW
91 BG	322, 323, 324, 401	7 Nov 1942	B-17	1 CBW
303 BG	358, 359, 360, 427	17 Nov 1942	B-17	41 CBW
305 BG	364, 365, 366, 422	17 Nov 1942	B-17	40 CBW
94 BG	331, 332, 333, 410	13 May 1943	B-17	4 CBW
95 BG	334, 335, 336, 412	13 May 1943	B-17	13 CBW
351 BG	508, 509, 510, 511	14 May 1943	B-17	94 CBW
96 BG	337, 338, 339, 413	14 May 1943	B-17	45 CBW
379 BG	524, 525, 526, 527	29 May 1943	B-17	41 CBW
381 BG	532, 533, 534, 535	22 Jun 1943	B-17	1 CBW
384 BG	544, 545, 546, 547	22 Jun 1943	B-17	41 CBW
100 BG	349, 350, 351, 418	25 Jun 1943	B-17	13 CBW
389 BG	564, 565, 566, 567	9 Jul 1943‡	B-24	2 CBW
388 BG	560, 561, 562, 563	22 Jul 1943	B-17	45 CBW
385 BG	548, 549, 550, 551	22 Jul 1943	B-17	4 CBW
390 BG	568, 569, 570, 571	12 Aug 1943	B-17	13 CBW
392 BG	576, 577, 578, 579	9 Sep 1943	B-24	14 CBW
482 BG	812, 813, 814	27 Sep 1943	B-17/B-24	
401 BG	612, 613, 614, 615	26 Nov 1943	B-17	94 CBW
445 BG	700, 701, 702, 703	13 Dec 1943	B-24	2 CBW
446 BG	704, 705, 706, 707	16 Dec 1943	B-24	20 CBW
448 BG	712, 713, 714, 715	22 Dec 1943	B-24	20 CBW
447 BG	708, 709, 710, 711	24 Dec 1943	B-17	4 CBW
453 BG	732, 733, 734, 735	5 Feb 1944	B-24	2 CBW
452 BG	728, 729, 730, 731	5 Feb 1944	B-17	45 CBW
457 BG	748, 749, 750, 751	21 Feb 1944	B-17	94 CBW
458 BG	752, 753, 754, 755	24 Feb 1944	B-24	96 CBW
466 BG	784, 785, 786, 787	22 Mar 1944	B-24	96 CBW
467 BG	788, 789, 790, 791	10 Apr 1944	B-24	96 CBW
398 BG	600, 601, 602, 603	6 May 1944	B-17	1 CBW

Bombardment Group	Bombardment Squadrons	Date Group Operational	A/c Type	Bombardment Wing
486 BG	832, 833, 834, 835	7 May 1944	B-24/B-17	92 CBW
487 BG	836, 837, 838, 839	7 May 1944	B-24/B-17	92 CBW
492 BG	856, 857, 858, 859	11 May 1944§	B-24	14 CBW
34 BG	4, 7, 18, 391	23 May 1944	B-24/B-17	93 CBW
489 BG	844, 845, 846, 847	30 May 1944	B-24	95 CBW
490 BG	848, 849, 850, 851	31 May 1944	B-24/B-17	93 CBW
491 BG	852, 853, 854, 855	2 Jun 1944	B-24	95 CBW
493 BG	860, 861, 862, 863	6 Jun 1944	B-24/B-17	93 CBW

*97 BG and 301 BG moved to North Africa with 12th AF Nov/Dec 1942.
†92 BG non-operational in an OTU role during period Oct 1942–Apr 1943.
‡389 BG first mission flown while on detachment in North Africa.
§492 BG assigned to special operations in Aug 1944.
482 BG operated both B-17 and B-24 and conducted experimental missions after spring 1944.
34, 486, 487, 490 and 493 BGs converted from B-24 to B-17 autumn 1944.

Heavy Bomber Units of the 15th Air Force
(*In order of entering combat*)

Bombardment Group	Bombardment Squadrons	Date Group Operational	A/c Type	Bombardment Wing
98 BG	343, 344, 345, 415	1 Aug 1942†	B-24	47 BW
97 BG	340, 341, 342, 414	17 Aug 1942†	B-17	5 BW
301 BG	32, 352, 353, 419	5 Sep 1942†	B-17	5 BW
376 BG	512, 513, 514, 515	1 Nov 1942*†	B-24	47 BW
99 BG	346, 347, 348, 416	31 Mar 1943†	B-17	5 BW
2 BG	20, 49, 96, 429	28 Apr 1943†	B-17	5 BW
449 BG	716, 717, 718, 719	8 Jan 1944	B-24	47 BW
450 BG	720, 721, 722, 723	8 Jan 1944	B-24	47 BW
451 BG	724, 725, 726, 727	30 Jan 1944	B-24	49 BW
454 BG	736, 737, 738, 739	8 Feb 1944	B-24	304 BW
456 BG	744, 745, 746, 747	10 Feb 1944	B-24	304 BW
455 BG	740, 741, 742, 743	12 Feb 1944	B-24	304 BW
459 BG	756, 757, 758, 759	2 Mar 1944	B-24	304 BW
463 BG	772, 773, 774, 775	16 Mar 1944	B-17	5 BW
460 BG	760, 761, 762, 763	19 Mar 1944	B-24	55 BW
461 BG	764, 765, 766, 767	2 Apr 1944	B-24	49 BW
483 BG	815, 816, 817, 840	12 Apr 1944	B-17	5 BW
484 BG	824, 825, 826, 827	29 Apr 1944	B-24	49 BW
464 BG	776, 777, 778, 779	30 Apr 1944	B-24	55 BW
465 BG	780, 781, 782, 783	5 May 1944	B-24	55 BW
485 BG	828, 829, 830, 831	10 May 1944	B-24	55 BW

*376 BG formed from provisional group that entered combat in June 1942
† 97 and 301 BGs commenced ops with 8 AF, 98 and 376 BGs with 9 AF, and 99 and 2 BGs with 12 AF.

Heavy Bombers and Crews on Hand in the 8th AF, August 1942 to May 1945

	Total Crews	B-17 Crews	B-24 Crews	Total H/B	B-17 A/c	B-24 A/c
1942						
Aug	39	39	—	104	104	—
Sep	76	—	—	178	144	34
Oct	128	—	—	296	234	62
Nov	205	—	—	247	180	67
Dec	176	—	—	219	178	41
1943						
Jan	155	—	—	214	175	39
Feb	146	—	—	255	186	69
Mar	190	—	—	303	229	74
Apr	231	—	—	590	502	88
May	340	—	—	705	599	93
Jun	455	408	47	846	783	51
Jul	596	553	43	856	820	24
Aug	806	613	193	907	786	109
Sep	933	708	225	971	835	96
Oct	1,116	796	320	1,138	907	197
Nov	1,960	1,427	533	1,554	1,166	294
Dec	2,081	1,472	609	1,686	1,302	308
1944						
Jan	2,147	1,479	668	1,817	1,341	433
Feb	2,163	1,429	734	1,998	1,412	553
Mar	2,155	1,285	870	2,295	1,487	772
Apr	2,496	1,461	1,035	2,647	1,492	1,070
May	3,225	1,715	1,510	3,137	1,502	1,435
Jun	3,550	1,816	1,734	3,100	1,471	1,458
Jul	3,996	2,291	1,705	3,492	1,695	1,609
Aug	4,000	2,392	1,608	3,662	1,829	1,606
Sep	3,671	2,412	1,259	3,659	1,927	1,471
Oct	3,587	2,348	1,239	3,818	2,143	1,330
Nov	3,686	2,407	1,279	3,795	2,123	1,321
Dec	3,869	2,553	1,316	3,706	2,168	1,183
1945						
Jan	3,925	2,615	1,310	3,534	2,125	1,077
Feb	4,201	2,746	1,455	3,702	2,269	1,066
Mar	4,204	2,850	1,354	3,761	2,367	1,045
Apr	3,760	2,587	1,173	3,688	2,291	1,041
May	2,718	2,029	689	2,958	1,988	719

Breakdown of B-17 and B-24 crews for period Sept 1942–May 1943 unavailable. Aircraft totals include replacements and second-line aircraft (training and restricted use) as well as those available for other than bombing duties. All figures are last day of month.

Heavy Bombers and Crews on Hand in the 15th AF, November 1943 to May 1945

	Total Crews	B-17 Crews	B-24 Crews	Total H/B	B-17 A/c	B-24 A/c
1943						
Nov	304	225	79	401	268	115
Dec	440	241	199	577	289	268
1944						
Jan	808	207	601	855	309	525
Feb	869	149	720	901	289	588
Mar	1,329	281	1,048	1,292	397	868
Apr	1,436	361	1,075	1,375	368	970
May	1,537	453	1,084	1,499	361	1,049
Jun	1,355	406	949	1,392	315	982
Jul	1,369	351	1,018	1,407	316	985
Aug	1,386	343	1,043	1,571	366	1,079
Sep	1,530	386	1,144	1,720	407	1,190
Oct	1,901	535	1,366	1,811	476	1,105
Nov	2,177	530	1,647	1,713	476	974
Dec	2,174	560	1,614	1,736	509	951
1945						
Jan	2,422	669	1,753	1,800	538	987
Feb	2,380	668	1,712	1,841	521	1,043
Mar	2,348	635	1,713	1,901	524	1,136
Apr	1,874	541	1,333	1,871	497	1,096
May	1,525	589	936	1,562	529	811

Aircraft totals include replacements and second-line aircraft (training and restricted use)
All figures are last day of month.

Tons of Bombs Dropped by 15th AF Heavy Bombers, November 1943 to May 1945

	High Explosive	Incendiary
1943		
Nov	5,392	—
Dec	7,752	—
1944		
Jan	11,051	—
Feb	6,611	136
Mar	9,842	534
Apr	20,657	599
May	29,606	749
Jun	23,637	829
Jul	30,621	1,562
Aug	27,660	179
Sep	20,645	211
Oct	15,712	545
Nov	16,153	1,144
Dec	18,308	449
1945		
Jan	6,784	—
Feb	24,417	91
Mar	30,265	—
Apr	29,181	77
May	84	—
	334,378	7,105

Grand total 341,483

Tons of Bombs Dropped by 8th AF Heavy Bombers, August 1942 to May 1945

	High Explosive	Incendiary
1942		
Aug	135	—
Sep	215	—
Oct	334	—
Nov	612	—
Dec	417	—
1943		
Jan	739	—
Feb	705	—
Mar	1,530	—
Apr	1,130	—
May	2,654	23
Jun	2,468	—
Jul	3,504	599
Aug	3,453	326
Sep	5,515	228
Oct	4,290	843
Nov	5,072	1,796
Dec	9,419	3,158
1944		
Jan	9,651	2,746
Feb	16,670	2,476
Mar	16,357	4,989
Apr	22,829	4,747
May	33,123	4,906
Jun	58,396	1,229
Jul	39,483	7,122
Aug	43,987	5,318
Sep	34,852	7,310
Oct	33,360	11,727
Nov	41,210	608
Dec	39,181	3,888
1945		
Jan	39,382	2,731
Feb	47,554	7,446
Mar	64,323	11,000
Apr	41,591	5,362
May	—	—
	624,141	90,578

Grand total 714,719

Airborne and Effective Combat Sorties, 8th AF Heavy Bombers

	Airborne	Effective
1942		
Aug	114	76
Sep	183	99
Oct	284	143
Nov	519	271
Dec	353	165
1943		
Jan	338	220
Feb	526	313
Mar	956	823
Apr	449	349
May	1,672	1,471
Jun	2,107	1,268
Jul	2,829	1,743
Aug	2,265	1,850
Sep	3,259	2,457
Oct	2,831	2,117
Nov	4,157	2,581
Dec	5,973	4,937
1944		
Jan	6,367	5,027
Feb	9,884	7,512
Mar	11,590	8,773
Apr	14,464	9,945
May	19,825	13,975
Jun	28,925	22,713
Jul	23,917	18,864
Aug	22,967	18,964
Sep	18,268	15,617
Oct	19,082	17,058
Nov	17,003	15,245
Dec	18,252	16,424
1945		
Jan	16,702	14,750
Feb	22,884	19,933
Mar	31,169	28,804
Apr	20,514	18,180
May	2,276	2,254
	332,904	274,921

May 1945 sorties chiefly food supply to Holland

Airborne and Effective Combat Sorties, 15th AF Heavy Bombers

	Airborne	Effective			
1943					
Nov	1,785	1,069	Sep	10,056	8,509
Dec	2,039	1,606	Oct	9,567	6,037
1944			Nov	9,259	6,955
Jan	4,720	3,811	Dec	10,050	7,235
Feb	3,981	2,380	*1945*		
Mar	5,996	4,202	Jan	4,002	2,918
Apr	10,182	8,084	Feb	13,444	10,748
May	14,432	11,584	Mar	14,939	12,737
Jun	11,761	10,001	Apr	15,846	11,771
Jul	12,642	10,825	May	42	36
Aug	12,194	10,760			
				166,937	131,268

8th AF Heavy Bomber Losses on Combat Missions, August 1942 to May 1945

	To E/A	To AA	Other Causes	Total
1942				
Aug	—	—	—	—
Sep	2	—	—	2
Oct	8	—	2	10
Nov	10	—	3	13
Dec	17	—	—	17
1943				
Jan	18	—	—	18
Feb	21	—	2	23
Mar	18	—	3	21
Apr	28	1	—	29
May	48	13	8	69
Jun	78	12	—	90
Jul	79	29	10	118
Aug	87	20	10	117
Sep	46	25	27	98
Oct	139	38	9	186
Nov	53	25	17	95
Dec	85	65	22	172
1944				
Jan	139	27	37	203
Feb	170	81	20	271
Mar	178	112	55	345
Apr	314	105	1	420
May	211	122	43	376
Jun	112	162	46	320
Jul	80	201	71	352
Aug	61	238	32	331
Sep	137	207	30	374
Oct	36	112	29	177

	To E/A	To AA	Other Causes	Total
Nov	50	146	13	209
Dec	28	74	17	119
1945				
Jan	49	222	43	314
Feb	14	157	25	196
Mar	63	164	39	266
Apr	72	77	41	190
May	1	4	2	7
	2,452	2,439	657	5,548

Non-operational losses not given
as no reliable source for totals exists

15th AF Heavy Bomber Losses on Combat Missions, November 1943 to May 1945

	To E/A	To AA	Other Causes	Total
1943				
Nov	25	1	2	28
Dec	30	3	3	36
1944				
Jan	20	10	24	54
Feb	106	11	11	128
Mar	42	19	24	85
Apr	105	65	24	194
May	50	107	18	175
Jun	85	79	32	196
Jul	94	170	53	317
Aug	91	112	51	254
Sep	7	71	16	94
Oct	—	110	30	140
Nov	1	69	62	132
Dec	18	110	77	205
1945				
Jan	—	46	42	88
Feb	—	108	39	147
Mar	7	93	49	149
Apr	—	65	18	83
May	—	9	5	14
	681	1,258	580	2,519

Non-operational losses not given as no reliable source for totals exists.
Other causes include losses due to mechanical failure, weather and
unknown causes.

Enemy Aircraft Claims Credited to 8th & 15th AF Heavy Bomber Gunners

	8th Air Force	15th Air Force
1942		
Aug	2	
Sep	16	
Oct	44	
Nov	47	
Dec	53	
1943		
Jan	45	
Feb	72	
Mar	142	
Apr	146	
May	372	
Jun	293	
Jul	527	
Aug	401	
Sep	255	
Oct	791	
Nov	106	84
Dec	231	128
1944		
Jan	582	135
Feb	397	230
Mar	363	105
Apr	346	429
May	380	242
Jun	42	226
Jul	98	336
Aug	23	122
Sep	65	13
Oct	12	—
Nov	29	3
Dec	61	48
1945		
Jan	41	—
Feb	1	—
Mar	23	9
Apr	92	—
May	—	—
	6,098	2,110

A total of 76,887,000 rounds of 0.50-in cal and 653,000 rounds of 0.30-in cal ammunition expended by 8th AF gunners and approx 30,000,000 rounds of 0.50-in cal by 15th AF gunners.

Very Heavy Bomber Units of the 20th AF
(*In order of entering combat*)

Bombardment Group	Bombardment Squadrons	Date Group Operational	Wing
40 BG	25, 44, 45, (395)	5 Jun 1944	
444 BG	676, 677, 678, (679)	5 Jun 1944	
462 BG	768, 769, 770 (771)	5 Jun 1944	58 BW
468 BG	792, 793, 794, (795)	5 Jun 1944	
497 BG	869, 870, 871	28 Oct 1944	
498 BG	873, 874, 875	28 Oct 1944	
500 BG	881, 882, 883	11 Nov 1944	73 BW
499 BG	877, 878, 879	24 Nov 1944	
505 BG	482, 483, 484	30 Dec 1944	
504 BG	398, 421, 680	16 Jan 1945*	
9 BG	1, 5, 99	25 Jan 1945	313 BW
6 BG	24, 39, 40	27 Jan 1945	
19 BG	28, 30, 93	12 Feb 1945	
29 BG	6, 43, 52	15 Feb 1945	
39 BG	60, 61, 62	6 Apr 1945	314 BW
330 BG	457, 458, 459	12 Apr 1945	
16 BG	15, 16, 17	16 Jun 1945	
501 BG	21, 41, 485	16 Jun 1945	
502 BG	402, 411, 430	30 Jun 1945	315 BW
331 BG	355, 356, 357	1 Jul 1945	
509 CG	393	1 Jul 1945	

*680 BS did not join 504 BG until June 1945
58 BW squadrons in brackets were all disbanded in Oct 1944

Very Heavy Bomber Losses 20th AF April 1944 to August 1945

	XX Bomber Command					XXI Bomber Command					
	To E/A	To AA	Other Causes	Total Combat	Non-Combat	To E/A	To AA	E/A & AA	Other Causes	Total Combat	Non-Combat
1944											
Apr	—	—	—	—	7*						
May	—	—	—	—	5						
Jun	1	—	9	10	8						
Jul	1	—	2	3	5						
Aug	3	1	10	14	5						
Sep	1	—	2	3	7						
Oct	1	—	4	5	16						
Nov	8	—	11	19	2	1	—	—	3	4	5
Dec	5	4	7	16	6	3	1	—	17	21	6
1945											
Jan	1	—	3	4	3	12	—	2	13	27	0
Feb	1	—	3	4	2	6	—	—	20	26	3
Mar	—	2	—	2	1	—	7	—	27	34	—
Apr						13	11	9	24	57	1
May						8	11	4	65	88	3
Jun						8	12	2	22	44	7
Jul						—	2	2	18	22	5
Aug						1	3	—	7	11	7
	22	7	51	80	67	52	47	19	216	334	38

Grand total 20th AF losses on combat missions 414 B-29s

20th AF non-combat losses   105 B-29s

Non-combat losses include those destroyed or scrapped after accidents.
Another ten B-29s were lost en route from the U.S.A. to combat theatres.

*Unconfirmed figure.

Very Heavy Bombers and Crews on Hand in the 20th AF, April 1944 to August 1945

	B-29	Crews	F-13	Crews		B-29	Crews	F-13	Crews
1944									
Apr	94	143	—	—	*1945*				
May	137	222	—	—	Jan	450	579	22	21
Jun	133	226	—	—	Feb	541	688	24	22
Jul	146	224	—	—	Mar	605	778	30	26
Aug	150	221	—	—	Apr	708	870	27	27
Sep	163	221	—	—	May	732	880	30	36
Oct	219	287	2	2	Jun	888	1,106	26	43
Nov	262	391	11	17	Jul	998	1,186	40	28
Dec	348	484	17	21	Aug	1,056	1,378	52	28

Includes first and second-line aircraft

Tons of Bombs Dropped by 20th AF

| | XX Bomber Command | | XXI Bomber Command | |
	High Explosive	Incendiary	High Explosive	Incendiary
1944				
Jun	501	46	—	—
Jul	209	—	—	—
Aug	184	68	—	—
Sep	521	—	—	—
Oct	1,023	646	—	—
Nov	1,415	215	343	232
Dec	1,556	—	1,495	610
1945				
Jan	1,584	422	927	477
Feb	1,261	604	1,140	1,015
Mar	1,019	417	3,086	10,761
Apr	—	—	13,209	4,283
May	—	—	6,937	17,348
Jun	—	—	9,954	22,588
Jul	—	—	9,388	33,163
Aug	—	—	8,438	12,591
	9,273	2,418	54,917	103,068

Grand totals 20th AF   High Explosive   64,190 ⎫
                        Incendiary   105,486 ⎬ 169,676
                                                 ⎭

Enemy Aircraft Claims Credited to 20th AF Very Heavy Bomber Gunners

	XX Bomber Command	XXI Bomber Command
1944		
Jun		
Jul		
Aug	18	
Sep	19	
Oct	21	
Nov	37	7
Dec	48	49
1945		
Jan	10	140
Feb	4	71
Mar	1	15
Apr		202
May		131
Jun		136
Jul		3
Aug		2
	158	756

A total of 11,368,000 rounds of 0.50-in cal and 32,000 rounds of 20 mm ammunition was expended by 20th AF gunners during combats